INVERSE

SAT PREP

THE CURSE

CARL CASCELLA

SAT PREP
INVERSE the CURSE
by
Carl Cascella

SAT PREP: Inverse the Curse

Copyright © 2014 Carl Cascella

All rights reserved.

ISBN:1-4942-8570-3

ISBN-13:978-1-4942-8570-8

Library of Congress Control Number: 2013921959

Dedication

To my students, for your enthusiasm and commitment.

To my many wonderful teachers, for your support and insights.

To those schools which recognize and nurture the unique talents of their students.

To my daughters, Ann and Christine, and to my wife, Theresa, for your love and encouragement.

Dear Barrett & Peggy —
Thanks for all the
great times together —
1972 - ∞ .
Love —
Carl

Preface

The wise Yogi Berra said, "You can observe a lot by just watching." Over the years as a test-taker and teacher, I've followed Yogi's advice. Here's what I've observed about the SAT:

- SAT questions are often different from those on high school exams.

- Students with the highest grades don't always have the highest SAT scores. Why?

- Overbearing parents and teachers aren't always as helpful as they think.

- After working on the SAT for a couple of hours, I noticed that my head throbbed and my eyes hurt. How do you solve this problem?

- The teacher in my high school who didn't encourage SAT prep held strenuous rehearsals before plays and concerts. Why didn't he believe in holding rehearsals for the SAT?

- Cool test takers have an advantage over those who become frenzied.

- Some SAT math questions concern topics that were covered years ago, as far back as grammar school. How do you remember these topics in the heat of taking the SAT?

- Trying to be perfect and being too competitive add to the pressure.
- Taking the SAT without prep work is like playing in the Super Bowl without a game plan.
- Those huge SAT textbooks can evoke almost as much fear as the test itself. How do you efficiently study *Barron's SAT* and still have time to do your regular homework?

Observations and questions like these challenged me to find solutions. The solutions, in turn, refined and enhanced my SAT prep classes and eventually prompted me to create this book.

As soon as I began to write *Inverse the Curse*, I realized that the world didn't need another monster SAT textbook such as those published by *Barron's*, the College Board, the Princeton Review, etc.

But, I am convinced that there **is** a place for an SAT prep book that addresses not only the facts, but also the physical and emotional stresses that the SAT generates. A ***guide*** that jump-starts your SAT prep and keeps you on course. A ***coach*** who shows you how to remain calm and focused so that all those years of schoolwork pay off in an SAT score that reflects your level of knowledge.

And, most of all, a ***counselor*** who reminds you that the SAT experience is all about **you**! What are your talents and your dreams? And, what path will best enable you to refine your talents so that you have the best chance to fulfill your dreams?

If I can help illuminate this path of discovery and fulfillment for you, then I believe that *SAT Prep: Inverse the Curse* will have been worth all the effort it took to produce.

With all my best wishes that you succeed on your journey, I remain—

Sincerely Yours,
Carl Cascella

TABLE OF CONTENTS

Part Four: Focus and Pacing-Timed Tests

Part Five: Developing Your SAT Strategy

Appendices

INTRODUCTION

INTRODUCTION
Mind, Body, Spirit—your SAT prep needs to cover all three

Face it. For most of us, the SAT is a mental, physical, and emotional grind. Doesn't it make sense, then, to work on all three areas—mind, body, and spirit—when you prep for the SAT?

As you read this book, you'll find ways to build your knowledge base (*mind*), to improve your stamina (*body*), and to boost your confidence (*spirit*) for all four subject areas covered on the SAT.

Most SAT prep books and courses focus on the "mind": the numbers, formulas, grammar, and vocab. Yes, of course, these are important. But, there are other critical factors that contribute to doing your best on the SAT.

There's the "body"—your *energy level*. How do you hold up during the long, stressful period that includes not only the actual SAT session, but also the days that lead up to SAT Saturday?

What's more, there's an *emotional* aspect to the SAT. How do you manage the emotional storm that the SAT can whip-up?

Have you ever felt an inner *pressure*- sometimes from your parents, sometimes from your teachers, but, most off all, the pressure you *put on yourself*? If so, you are not alone.

Dealing with this emotional turbulence is a critical aspect of SAT prep that this book covers but which many other books and prep courses do not.

Does SAT prep help? It's a common question to which I reply, "If I didn't think that my SAT prep worked, I wouldn't be doing it!"

When I took the SAT's and then later the GRE (like the SAT, but for admission to graduate school), the verbal section was my stumbling block. My verbal score didn't change – both in high school and after college. I was "capped" at the exact same point!

The problem that confronted me was that I had to score at least ninety points higher to be admitted into my top-choice graduate program.

Deep down, I knew that I could do better. Why wasn't I? As my test date approached, this question tormented me. Then, one fall afternoon while lap swimming, I went into focus mode and came up with a game plan that worked. Using the card method for vocab and the *Inverse the Curse* tool for critical reading, I was able to increase my verbal score by more than ninety points.

I tell you this because if I can do it, so can you!

You are most effective when your mind, body and spirit are all working at their highest levels. It's called "being in the zone." That's my goal: to have you in peak form–*as prepared as you can be*–on SAT Saturday. Let's get started!

PART ONE:
GETTING STARTED

HERE'S WHAT YOU NEED TO GET STARTED
Get hold of these and you're set to begin your prep

Here's your shopping list. You don't need anything expensive or exotic to get started: $45 should cover everything you need, including this book. Once you've collected the items on this list, you'll be set to begin your SAT prep.

- A one-subject notebook
- #2 Pencils, about a dozen. Use eight for your prep work and keep four of them for your SAT.
- Two pens, blue or black ink
- 3 X 5 inch index cards, with lines on one side. These come in packs of 100 cards. You'll need five packs.
- Elastic bands, a dozen of various sizes & colors
- Calculator. Use the *same calculator* for this prep and for your SAT so that you get used to its operation.
- *Barron's SAT,* by Green and Wolf

In my live SAT prep classes, I give each student a copy of *Barron's SAT*, which has two versions: standard and CD-rom. I suggest the standard (non CD- rom) edition. ***That's the text I'll use as the primary reference for this book and which I suggest that you use to begin your preparation for the SAT.***

After you have finished this course, you may want to explore other excellent SAT guides, such as *Cracking the SAT*, by the Princeton Review, and *The Official SAT Study Guide*, by the College Board. The work you do with me here in *SAT Prep* will be enable you to zip through these two texts and to extract more from them.

Barron's, though, is a terrific starting point. It includes step-by-step solutions for both the practice and sample SAT questions. This is helpful because you can check your own work against the solutions in *Barron's*. You'll understand why you may be off target and you will be able to correct your work because the solutions are clearly illustrated.

Barron's SAT also provides you with excellent math, grammar, and vocab review sections. ***We'll set up a schedule that directs you to key pages in "Barron's" so that you don't waste valuable time wondering what to do and when to do it.***

I recommend a hard copy of *Barron's*. You can use my small book and index cards when you are on the go; and, you can use your big SAT textbook at home or school where you can spread out, take notes, mark-up the book, etc. Being able to work at a desk ***and*** on the go will help you save time as you fit-in your SAT prep with all the other activities you want to do.

So, with your tools in hand, let's begin!

YOUR SCHEDULE HELPS YOU STAY ON COURSE
Taking it one day at a time reduces stress and improves efficiency

Last week, my daughter was stressing about having to study for the SAT and, at the same time, having to apply to college. There were so many details swirling in her mind that she became confused and overwhelmed.

"Take it one step at a time," I told her. "Think of how the Egyptians built the pyramids, and do the same thing for your SAT prep: one brick at a time."

To reduce your stress and to stay on course, set up a schedule similar to the one I'll outline for you. My sample schedule is for 10 weeks, the duration of my SAT prep classes. But, you can alter this ten-week schedule to fit your own timetable. Simply allocate your time according to these guidelines:

- **20% Memory**—you construct cards which reinforce key concepts for all sections of the test.

- **60% Review**—you work on practice SAT questions one at a time to become familiar with the test's format and style.

- **20% Timed Tests**—you do timed sections designed like the actual test to get used to SAT pacing and time management.

If you have a ten-week schedule, this means that you'll spend the first two weeks creating your index cards, what I call the **Memory** work. This is the background information you'll need to know in order to answer the kinds of questions that appear on the SAT.

Then, for the next six weeks, you will do **Review Questions** in your big SAT textbook. During your review, you work on one question at a time, making sure that you understand the concepts.

For the final two weeks, your **Timed Tests** will show you how to manage your time during the actual test. You'll learn how to pace yourself and how to improve your focus and stamina.

You can adapt this schedule to accommodate any number of weeks you will devote to your SAT prep. If your timetable is five weeks, set-up your prep like this.

- Week 1: memory
- Weeks 2-3-4: review questions
- Week 5: timed tests.

For a longer time frame—say sixteen weeks— spend the first three weeks on memory, the next ten weeks on review questions, and the final three weeks on timed tests.

The key is to *set-up your schedule by writing it on the first page of your notebook.*

Your written schedule will guide you day-by-day, week-by-week, right up to SAT Saturday. *Your schedule will keep you moving forward and on course.* It will focus you. And, by being focused on your work, you will have less time to worry. *By following the schedule, you will feel more in control and less anxious.*

The chart outlines a 10-week SAT prep routine. I will explain the entire schedule to you, starting with Week 1: Math Facts 1-25. Let's get started there!

Schedule for Barron's SAT

Week	Math	Vocabulary	Writing/Reading	Essay Theme Cards
1	Facts 1-25	A B C	Cards 286-291	History
2	Facts 26-50	D E F	Cards 292-298	Current Events
3	Review A B	G H I J	Pages 265-285	Science - Past & Current
4	Review C D E	K L M N O	Pages 299-318	Psychology
5	Review F G H	P Q R	Pages 319-340	Sports
6	Review I J K	S T U	Pages 91-105	Literature Drama Poetry
7	Review L M N	V W X Y Z	Pages 107-142	Biography Quotes
8	Review O P Q R	All A-Z	All Cards	Art Music Film
9	Read Pages 3-26 and do Timed Test 1			
10	Timed Test 2			

PART TWO:
KEY BACKGROUND MATERIAL FOR THE SAT

MEMORY FOR MATH
Use your schedule to stay on course

So far, you have amassed your materials: pens, index cards, *Barron's SAT* textbook, etc. And, you have set-up a schedule that works for you. What's next?

Using your schedule as a guide, let's start with memory for math. Then, we'll move across the top line of the schedule for memory assignments in vocab, writing/reading, and the essay.

Your first activity is to create index cards for the ***"50 Essential Math Facts"*** listed in Appendix A. If you follow the 10-week schedule, that means you'll make 25 cards per week.

Here's how to proceed. First, write the name of the math fact on the unlined side of your 3×5 index card. Then, flip the card over and re-write the name followed by its definition. ***Be sure to use a pen when you create your cards so that they don't smudge.*** Annotate your cards as you construct them and as you work on your practice problems. Your own notes will help you to remember terms and concepts.

Once you're finished making the cards, memorize them. Read the terms on the back of the cards, and see if you can accurately define them. Check yourself by flipping the cards over and reading the definitions.

When I was studying for test, I carried the cards with me at all times. Whenever I had a couple of idle minutes, I'd study them. You'll find that very short (3 to 5 minute) sessions with the cards help to reinforce the terms. Make good use of your free moments throughout the day to practice with the cards. This really works!

The math cards are concise definitions that are the first step in your math prep. After you have constructed and memorized the essential math facts, you will be ready to begin practice problems. Then, you'll see how ***this background memory work will help you solve the kind of math questions that appear on the SAT.***

Let's get started with Card 1, whose title is "Integer." Using a pen, write 1. Integer on the unlined side of the card.

1. Integer

Write the name of the term on the back (unlined) side of your index card

Then, flip the card over and write:

1. Integer

Any number that does not contain either a fraction or a decimal.

…-5, -4, -3, -2, -1, 0, 1, 2, 3, 4, 5…

Note: integers can be negative, positive, or 0.

---

1. Integer

Any # that does **not** contain
a fraction or a decimal

... -5, -4, -3, -2, -1, 0, 1, 2, 3, 4, 5...

Note: Integers **can** be +, -, or 0

For your geometry cards, it helps to draw figures and to make notes to help you remember key terms. Use the blank side of your index card to draw your diagram. Then, define the terms on the lined side of the card.

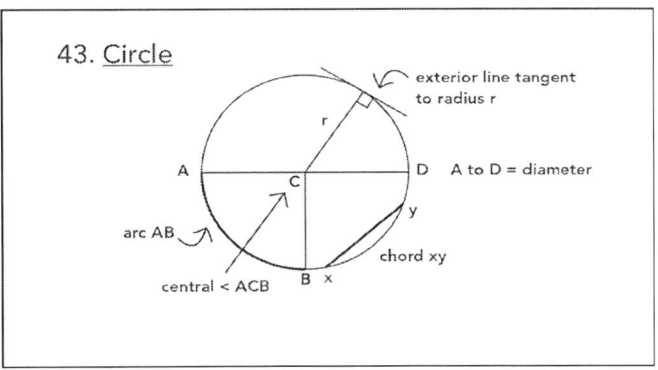

43. Circle

exterior line tangent to radius r

A to D = diameter

arc AB

chord xy

central < ACB

---

43. Circle
contains 360°
D= diameter= 2x radius (r)
Area= πr^2
Circumference= πD or $2\pi r$
π= C÷D=~3.14
*Longest chord= diameter
*Exterior line tangent to a radius forms a right angle
Length of an arc= (central angle÷360°) x circumference
Area of sector= (central angle÷360°) x total area of circle

Summary of Instructions—Memory for Math

- Start your SAT prep routine by making index cards for the "50 Essential Math Facts," which you will find in Appendix A at the end of this book.

- Use a pen so that the cards don't smudge.

- Annotate cards to reinforce the definitions. Use your own shorthand, as I did in the Circle card, above.

- Consult *Barron's* Chapter 9 (Pages 409-628) to clarify any unfamiliar terms.

- Carry the cards with you and memorize them in short spurts throughout the day.

MEMORY FOR VOCAB
Vocab drills are routines like lifting weights, running sprints, and practicing scales

Once you're up and running with the math cards, you can begin the next phase of your memory prep: vocabulary. Your schedule breaks vocab memory into manageable pieces. You'll spend about twenty minutes a day for the first seven weeks of your prep covering the entire alphabet. That will leave you about three weeks at the end to master any troublesome words.

Building your vocab is one of the most effective tactics to improve your critical reading and writing scores. It's like lifting weights for athletes, or practicing scales for musicians. ***You get into a rhythm of doing your routines every day;*** and, after a couple of weeks, you find that your muscles have developed and that your "game" has improved.

The *Barron's SAT* really shines in terms of vocab. *Barron's* contains flash cards for over 200 key words.

That's your priority: ***memorize those cards.*** There's also a comprehensive word list in *Barron's SAT* which you can tackle once you've mastered the cards.

To get started, separate the perforated yellow cards at the back of the book, and you're ready to go. Week 1 on the schedule specifies that you cover letters A-B-C. Divide your A-B-C flash cards into two stacks: familiar and unfamiliar.

Put an elastic band around the unfamiliar stack, and hammer away at those words. ***Once you've mastered an unfamiliar word, move it from the unfamiliar stack into the familiar stack.***

Work the same way in Week 2: separate D-E-F words into familiar and unfamiliar, and then focus on the unfamiliar stack (which still might contain words from Week 1).

When I practiced like this, my unfamiliar stack contained about 75 words at the end of Week 7. I concentrated on those 75 words for the next three weeks. By test time, there were only 17 words remaining in the unfamiliar stack.

One of those unfamiliar words was on the test – can you believe it! I had the cards in my pocket and studied them as I rode the subway to the test center. As a result, I remembered the definition and got it right on the test. The word was *descry.*

Summary of Instructions—Memory for Vocab

Vocab building is easy—there's no need for high-level thinking. But, it takes a while because there are so many words to cover. The key is to follow your schedule so that you make every day count.

Carry your pack of unfamiliar vocab cards with you and study them whenever you can. Short spurts work the best. This constant repetition worked for me as it has worked for many of my students.

One final hint: it helps to make notes, pictures, or quotes on your cards, as I've done on this sample card.

```
Optimism
     n. hopefulness, confidence +
     vs. pessimism = negativism -

     "Optimism is a force multiplier,"
     says former Secretary of State Colin
     Powell, because it strengthens  you.

     adj. optimistic
```

MEMORY FOR WRITING SKILLS
How to spot grammatical gaffes such as should-a, could-a, would-a

The writing skills section of the SAT will test your knowledge of grammar and usage. Since you've already learned most of this material, your review should move along quickly once you set up the system I suggest.

Barron's comes through with three terrific word listings that cover much of what you need for the SAT's multiple-choice writing questions:

- **Words Often Misused or Confused** (Page 286)

- **Picking Proper Prepositions** (Page 292)

- **Irregular Verbs** (Page 296)

Your Week 1 and 2 Schedules assign you to review these lists and to make index cards for any unfamiliar words. Follow the same procedure as you are doing with your math and vocab cards: construct the cards during Weeks 1 and 2, carry them with you, and memorize them over the next eight weeks of your prep schedule.

There are 44 words in *Barron's* "Misused or Confused" listing, starting around Page 286. Here's how one of my own cards is set up.

The blank side of the card contains the terms you need to memorize.

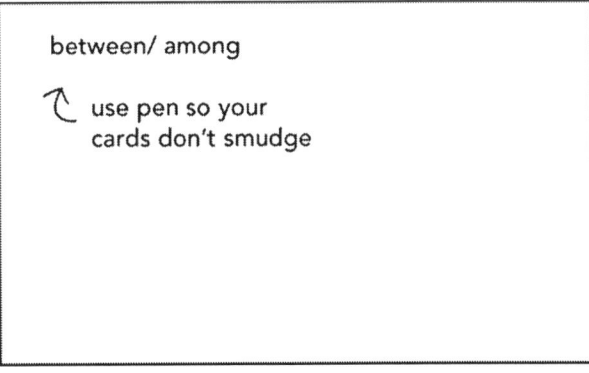

Flip your card over, and write the definitions onto the lined side of the card. To help you remember the definitions, include your own notes and illustrations.

```
  between/among

    between - refers to 2

    among - refers to more than 2

    ex. between you and me
        among Jean, you, and me


```

Your goal is to *be sure that you can nail these definitions*. Be honest with yourself. If you're not certain of a term, make and memorize a card for it.

The second listing, "Picking Proper Prepositions," will help you spot usage errors involving prepositions. *Barron's* list on Page 292 begins with the phrase *accede to*. You need to know both the definition of the verb and the preposition that follows it.

You should be able to buzz through *Barron's* listing of "Irregular Verbs," starting with *arise-arose- arisen* on Page 296. Again, make and memorize cards for any irregular verbs that are unfamiliar to you.

Summary of Instructions: Memory for Writing Skills

As I said earlier, you should find this material easy to review. You just need to set up your card system and get started. For the first two weeks of your 10-week review, you'll need just fifteen minutes a day to construct your cards for all three lists. Then, you'll have the remaining eight weeks to memorize them.

Pacing yourself is the key to this process. Think of your prep as a marathon—not a sprint. By doing a little every day, you will **avoid the cramming frenzy** that ensnares many test takers. Taking action— making the cards—will have positive side effects. ***The very act of creating your cards will aid your memorization process and reduce your stress!***

MEMORY FOR THE ESSAY
Yes, there is a way you can prep for the essay

There is a mistaken notion that you cannot prepare for the SAT essay assignment. This is not true. You *can* prep for the essay using a technique I call the ***Adjustable Wrench***, devised after my daughter Ann took her first SAT. Here's what happened.

After writing about a third of her essay, Ann became alarmed that she was taking the "wrong" point of view. So, she erased what she had written and started over again.

This, of course, wasted precious minutes. Then, while she was doing her re-write, Ann realized that she probably wouldn't have enough time to finish it. She became frantic and froze, her mind becoming a blank.

Ann was losing control, going into a kind of mental overdrive. After a couple of minutes, she was able to resume writing. But she was not addressing the topic. Instead of sticking to the assignment, Ann began writing about Catholic doctrine, stuff that she had memorized year after year in Sunday school.

In other words, Ann was in speed mode and was writing about ideas that were most familiar to her, concepts that had been drilled into her head and which came to the surface when she was stressed. Her page was full of writing; but her work didn't relate to the assignment!

As Ann relayed her story to me, I became dismayed. I wanted to help her, but I didn't know how.

Then, a most amazing and lucky thing occurred. Yale's *a cappella* group, *Baker's Dozen*, performed at Ann's high school. After the concert, Ann called me and said, "*Baker's Dozen* just sang one of your favorite songs, *Loch Lomond*. Do you know what it's about, Dad?"

Since I knew the lyrics… *Where me and my true love will never meet again…* I said, "Of course I do. It's about two lovers who have become separated."

"Dad, you're way off base," Ann said. "The Yalies told us that *Loch Lomond* is about two Scottish brothers captured by the English during the Scottish War for Independence. The English wanted to make an example of these brothers to intimidate the Scots. So, they killed one in full view of the other, and then allowed the surviving brother to return home, to Scotland."

Ann's story surprised me. I had extracted the obvious theme from the lyrics; the true meaning was far different from what I thought.

Then, for some reason, ***I related my misunderstanding of "Loch Lomond" to Ann's frustration during her SAT essay assignment.***

"You should make an index card about this," I told Ann. "The theme is *What is obvious is not necessarily what is true.*" The ballad was obviously about two lovers; the lyrics, however, were really telling the story of two brothers, one executed, the other grief-stricken.

"Make a lot of cards like this on all kinds of topics," I suggested to Ann, "and use these cards as background material for your SAT essay."

Several months later, Ann took her second SAT. By then, I had forgotten about the Loch Lomond theme card idea. Right after the test, though, Ann called me. I could tell that she was excited and upbeat.

"Dad, you're not going to believe this," she said. "The essay assignment was like the *Loch Lomond* theme card, something like *What is obvious is not always what is correct.*"

This was one of those ah-ha moments. **Inspiration: I would have my students create a variety of theme cards**-just like Ann's *Loch Lomond* card-***to use as background material for their SAT essays.***

I called this the ***Adjustable Wrench*** technique because—like an adjustable wrench that can tighten bolts of many sizes—it's a tool that you can use on a ***wide range*** of SAT essay assignments.

The key is to ***create cards that cover all kinds of subjects***. By having an assortment of theme cards, you will increase your chances of having at least one card that you can relate to the SAT. No one knows what the next essay assignment will be; but, by creating a variety of theme cards, you'll have plenty of background material to use no matter what the SAT throws at you.

In class, we make theme cards on science, politics, art, psychology, business, sports, music, mythology, philosophy, history, literature, current events, and cinema. You name it!

We quote political figures, artists, inventors, athletes, writers, musicians, and scientists including Steve Jobs, Winston Churchill, Walt Disney, Tom Hanks, Michael Jordan, and Mark Twain.

Here's one on Winston Churchill, who said, *"An appeaser is someone who feeds a crocodile hoping it will eat him last."*

Churchill, on Appeasers
"An appeaser is one who feeds a crocodile hoping it will eat him last."
Winston Churchill, British Statesman

Appeasement= policy followed by Brit Prime Minister Neville Chamberlain= making concessions to Hitler to avoid military conflict<WWII 1935 to 1939 Chamberlain signed "Munich Agreement"

---

30 Sept 1938 permitting Nazi Germany to annex areas of Czechoslovakia called the "Sudetenland."
Churchill warned Brits + French that appeasing Hitler would not work. But Europe was war-weary and did not listen to WC. They wanted **"peace at any price."** Sept 1939 Hitler invades Poland. Brits declare war on Germany.
WC's warnings proved correct. Churchill becomes Prime Minister and leads England to victory in WWII.

Notice that my card contains Churchill's quote, plus its setting, or context. You can see that I use my own shorthand, like the = and < signs. Do the same on your cards, ***using your own shorthand and including details that you can work into your writing.***

For example, this Churchill card provides material for SAT essay assignments such as these:

Assignment I. "War is not an effective means to resolve international crises. When one nation threatens another, the best solution is to seek reconciliation and to avoid armed conflict at any cost." Do you agree or disagree with this statement? Support you viewpoint, using examples from your studies and/or your experiences.

Assignment II. "When one nation threatens another, the only effective solution is a military response. The cultural and philosophic differences among nations have rendered diplomacy an ineffective means to resolve international crises."

Compose an essay in which you express your points of view on this statement. Your essay may support or refute the views expressed in the statement.

If essay assignments like this appear on the SAT, you could use the Churchill card as background material. ***Your card would provide a spark to get you started***, just as Ann's *Loch Lomond* card did for her. ***Having this material in mind keeps your pencil moving, quells your anxiety, and adds depth and interest to your writing!***

Here are some theme cards that we've composed in my SAT class:

- How Willis Carrier's invention of the ***air conditioner*** in 1902 encouraged the migration to the Sunbelt and prompted the construction of skyscrapers in New York City. Can you imagine living in Florida or working in a skyscraper without air conditioning?

This card directly illustrates how scientific discoveries alter our lives. You could also include another and more obvious example of the ***relationship between science and society*** by citing how the computer and the Internet are affecting us today.

- Daniel Goleman's terrific book, *Emotional Intelligence*, from which we quote: "From the standpoint of emotional intelligence, ***optimism*** is an attitude that buffers people against falling into apathy, hopelessness, or depression in the face of tough going."
  General Colin Powell said, "Optimism is a force multiplier."
  Yogi Berra said, "Baseball is 90% mental; the other half is physical."
  Relate these three quotes to a topic like ***what is the relation between mindset and success?***

- The **Ponzi Scheme**, a financial fraud name after swindler Charles Ponzi in 1907. The most notorious Ponzi Scheme, perpetrated by Bernie Madoff in 2009, created global economic upheaval. Why do supposedly intelligent people fall for Ponzi Schemes year after year? Why can't the government regulators detect and disable Ponzi Schemes before they damage the financial system?

- Pavlov's notion of ***stimulus and response***, derived from his experiment with the salivating dog. Are we humans governed by similar "conditioned responses," or has mankind evolved beyond such primitive behavior?

- Portia's plea for mercy in *The Merchant of Venice.* "The quality of mercy is not strained. It droppeth as the gentle rain from heaven upon the place beneath... And earthly power most resembles God's when mercy seasons justice." You can relate what Portia said to an SAT topic such as "Should our justice system operate according to the harsh principle of an *eye for an eye,* or should justice be tempered with mercy?"

Pick your own themes for the cards. ***Write about things that interest you.*** That's important. When you're done with your 24 cards, you might discover that your themes have a common thread... and that common thread is ***you***!

Just a couple of ground rules: do not use the same topics I've mentioned. Pick other themes. And, avoid cards about the "Big 5": Washington, Lincoln, Kennedy, King, and whoever is the current President. These are the most common citations I read on my students' essays. ***Set yourself apart from the crowd by including new and interesting facts that may add interest and appeal to your writing... and which may dazzle your graders!***

To get you started on making your own cards, follow these steps to create a card titled **"Rembrandt vs. Matisse."** First, Google search "Rembrandt Self-Portrait 1634" and "Matisse Portrait of Madame Matisse 1903." With those two paintings in mind, research the artists—their lives, their times, their theories on art, and other examples of their work. Then, distill this information onto two sides of an index card.

Rembrandt vs.	Matisse
self-portrait 1634	Portrait Madame Matisse 1903

Rembrandt 1606-1669

Dutch "old master"

Style=representational

Detailed, three-dimensional

Full tonal range from deep shadows

to bright highlights

Color not vivid=muted

Classical composition

Matisse- 1869-1954

French-Fauvist School

In French, "fauve" means "wild beast"

Considered savage by the art world

Shocking use of color was not initially embraced

because it was not realistic

Said "Exactitude is not truth."

Sought to create emotion through vivid use of

color. Very bright lighting. Now recognized as a

leading figure in history of art.

You could use this theme card for SAT essay assignments like these:

Assignment I. "In 1899, the head of the US Patent Office, Charles H. Duell, said that *Everything that can be invented has been invented.*" What are your thoughts on Duell's statement? Do you agree or disagree with it?

Assignment II. "What is truly innovative resides in the realm of the sciences. All other human endeavors appear stagnant when compared to the advances that have occurred in science and technology." Comment on this statement, using examples based on your studies and/or your experience.

Assignment III. "The definition of beauty is fixed, never changing. Aesthetics, like truth, is a constant from one era to the next." Compose an essay in which you express your views on this topic. Your essay may support, refute, or *qualify* the views expressed in the above quotation.

Note that the word "*qualify*" means that you agree with the quotation in some circumstances, and disagree with it in other circumstances. *You limit—or "qualify"—your point of view by citing specific examples of when you agree and when you disagree with the statement.*

Summary of Instructions—Memory for the Essay

Here's what to do now.

- Create three theme cards per week for Weeks 1-8.

- Use a pen so your cards won't smudge.

- Work on both sides of the card. Include details and quotes to add interest and appeal to your topics.

- *Vary your topics* as suggested on the schedule.

- Memorize your cards so that you know them by heart, just as you know the words of your favorite songs.

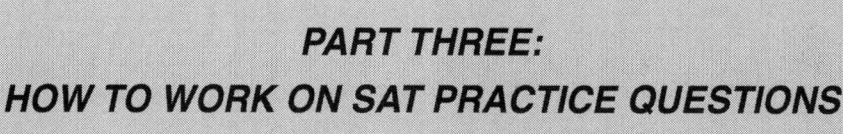

PART THREE:
HOW TO WORK ON SAT PRACTICE QUESTIONS

MOVING INTO THE REVIEW SECTION OF YOUR SAT PREP

Your memory work will save you time, trouble, and money. You *gotta know* that a **circle contains 360 degrees** and that **2 is the only even prime number.** You *gotta know* the difference between **accept** and **except**, and that long lines at Starbucks are **irritating**—not **aggravating**. And, you must know that *gotta know* is non-standard and that you should avoid using it on the SAT!

Some students think that re-taking the SAT several times will automatically raise their scores. But, think about it. This could cost you time and money and not necessarily help you. Re-taking the SAT could, as Yogi Berra said, simply reinforce "bad mistakes." If you don't know the key background material, you will probably repeat the same mistakes from one SAT to another. You'd just be spinning your wheels!

Instead of worrying about when and how many times you should take the SAT, do this. Hammer away at your prep schedule, and take your first SAT. Jot down your problem areas and re-study them. This process could take a month or two. After you've ironed out your difficulties, then you will be ready for your second SAT.

Let's get back to your prep schedule. Now that you've completed most of the memory assignments, it's time to begin review questions. The Week 3-8 schedule directs you to specific pages in *Barron's* where you will find practice questions for the math, critical reading, and writing skills sections of the SAT.

Note that the **Schedule for Vocab** and **Essay** for **Weeks 3-8** is the same format as for Weeks 1-2: you simply move down the alphabet for vocab and compose more theme cards for the essay.

Follow these guidelines when you work on review questions:

- Always *use pencil*...because that's what you'll do on the SAT

- Use the *same calculator* as you will on the test...so that you are familiar with its operation

- *Work on one question at a time.* After you solve it, refer to the "Answer Explanations" in *Barron's* to be sure that you are correct. This will prevent you from repeating errors in your solution process. *Correct errors ASAP in order not to reinforce them.*

- Read the entire Review Section of this book before you begin working on SAT review questions in *Barron's*. You'll find tips and techniques in the next few pages designed to improve your score.

- As you work on SAT practice questions, *go for accuracy, not for speed.*

Have you ever stared at a math question, perplexed and frozen, not knowing how to begin? Or, have you ever revved-up to such a frenzied state that you became frantic and out of control?

I admit that I have had similar reactions to SAT math questions. And, I know from experience that once you begin to react—either by becoming frozen or frenzied—that you are at a big disadvantage. Reacting rarely works on the SAT (or anywhere else in life) because once you are in a re-active state, you are at the mercy of the annoying force that takes away your self-control.

On practice tests, I have seen students staring into space, not knowing how to begin; and, I've watched them furiously writing, erasing, and re-starting, punching calculator keys and shaking their heads as their ears turn red.

I also experienced the red-ear syndrome during my SAT, so don't get down on yourself if you have also shared this distress! The good news is that there is a solution, a way to get your emotions in check and to regain your composure.

To maintain your self-control and to move forward, I suggest an approach called the *Catalyst Technique*. You may know the term "catalyst" from your chem class. It's a substance that encourages a reaction.

Similarly, on the SAT, the ***catalyst is the spark that gets you started on course to your solution.***

There are five catalysts, which are arranged to take into account the progression of the questions on the math sections of the SAT. The questions in *Barron's* practice tests and the actual SAT math sections are arranged in order of difficulty: easy to medium to difficult as you move forward from question 1 up to question 20.

You'll use Catalysts 1 and 2 on the simple math questions; Catalysts 2, 3 and 4 on the medium questions; and Catalysts 4 and 5 on the difficult ones.

Remember: the purpose of these catalysts is to ***get your pencil moving*** in the right direction. By using the *Catalyst Technique*, you will avoid the temptation to solve these tricky math SAT questions "in your head." Your emotions will stay in check, and your accuracy will improve!

Catalyst #1: Solve for x.

Example: If $x+2= 6$, what is $4x + 9$?
Solution: solve for x, then plug-in.
$x = 4$
Therefore, $4x + 9 = 25$

Hint: When solving easy math questions, you may be tempted to set up complicated and unnecessary one-step equations. This will waste time. Instead, go for the simple and direct solution. Solve for x, then, plug-in x to arrive at the answer.

Catalyst #2: Fill-in data, then solve.

For the easy-medium questions, the SAT usually provides a diagram, as in this question from *Barron's* Practice Test 1, Section 3.

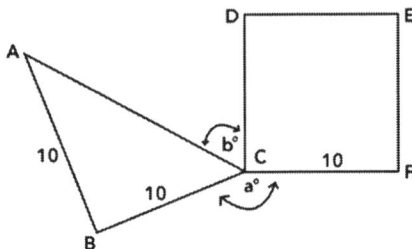

Question: In the figure above, C is the only point that right triangle ABC and square CDEF have in common. What is the value of a+b?

Here's how to get started.

First, quickly read the question. Scan the diagram. Then, go back and read the question *slowly*, stopping to *fill-in as much data as soon you can.*

As soon as you read *"right triangle ABC,"* stop reading, and *go right to the diagram. Indicate the 90° angle in the triangle.*

When you do, you'll see that this triangle has two sides of **length 10**. Two equal sides translate into two equal opposite angles.

You have an isosceles right triangle with angles of 90°-45°-45°. *Write that into your diagram*, which should now look like this.

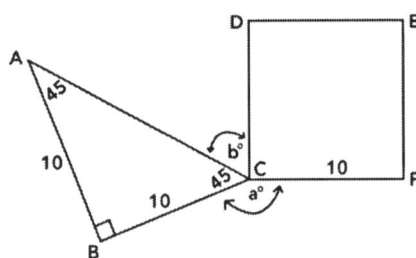

Resume reading the question, which refers to "*square CDEF.*" **Indicate the 90-degree angle** for square *CDEF* at Point C.

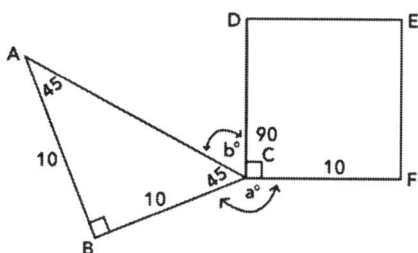

By writing-in this information, you can more easily spot the solution. Don't you see the circle with central angles of a°, b°, 45°, and 90°?

Knowing that circles contain 360°, *you set-up your equation*:

$$a° + b° + 45° + 90° = 360°$$
$$a° + b° = 360° - 135°$$
$$a° + b° = \mathbf{225°}$$

For SAT math questions, proceed like this and you will be rewarded! ***Fill-in as much data as you can, as soon as you can.*** Mark-up your diagram. Get your pencil moving! Then, the solution will present itself to you. ***What you jot-down in your test book creates a trail which leads you to the answer.*** If you follow the logic of these solution steps, you are on your way to improving your SAT math score. Re-read this section to be sure you fully understand it. It's important!

Catalyst #3: Draw a diagram, fill-in data, and solve

The difference between Catalyst 3 and Catalyst 2 is that no diagram is provided for C3. You have to draw it. Then, work just as we did for C2. Fill-in as much data as you can, write a formula, and solve the question.

Example: A circle is inscribed in a square whose sides are 4 inches. What is the area of the circle?

First, draw your diagram

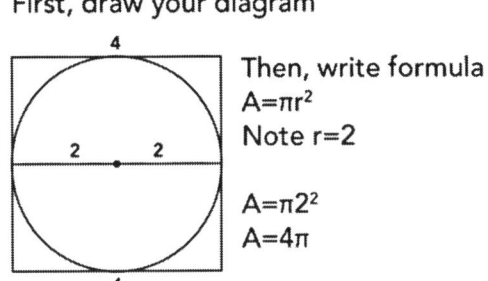

Then, write formula
$A=\pi r^2$
Note $r=2$

$A=\pi 2^2$
$A=4\pi$

Be sure to take the time to draw a diagram and to write the formula for the area of a circle. By doing so, you will increase the odds of being correct. Having the diagram and the formula in sight will enable you to focus on the data without the strain of juggling all the numbers in your mind. As you work in this manner, you'll find that you will minimize errors and improve your accuracy. Plus, it's easier and quicker for you to check your work once it's written down in the test booklet.

Catalyst # 4: Transform a Complicated Question into a Simple Diagram or Equation.

In Catalyst #3, your diagrams involve usual geometric forms: lines, angles, rectangles, circles, etc. As the math questions progress to the higher-numbered questions (which increase in difficulty), you may be asked to solve unusual questions that involve people standing in lines, sitting in buses, walking across fields, working on assembly lines, etc.

No problem! Simply sketch a diagram. Nothing elaborate. The purpose of the diagram is to show you a visual clue that leads to your solution.

This question is taken from *Barron's* Practice Test 4, Section 7.

Question: A school group charters three identical buses and occupies ⅘ of the seats. After ¼ of the passengers leave, the remaining passengers use only two of the buses. What fraction of the seats on the two buses are now occupied?

Catalyst: Draw a simple diagram of three buses. Here's my version…featuring the new VW hybrid minibus.

4 of 5 seats occupied. Thus, 12 passengers.
¼ leave. ¼ of 12 = 3 passengers leave. Thus, 9 remain.
There are 10 seats on two buses.
9 passengers/10 seats = 9/10 occupied

Catalyst #5: Multi-step Solution

The most difficult math questions will generally involve several steps. You ***solve them in stages*** by using several of the techniques from Catalysts 1-4.

The trick here is to avoid the temptation for a quick, one-step solution. Instead, take your time and do one step at a time, working with a diagram or an equation rather than trying to solve the question in your head.

Here's an example from *Barron's* Practice Test 3, Section 8.

> **If A is 25 kilometers east of B, which is 12 kilometers south of C, which is 9 kilometers west of D, how far, in kilometers, is A from D?**

Start by drawing your diagram. Label the lengths of the line segments. By putting your work on paper, you are on your way to finding the solution! Here's how my diagram looks.

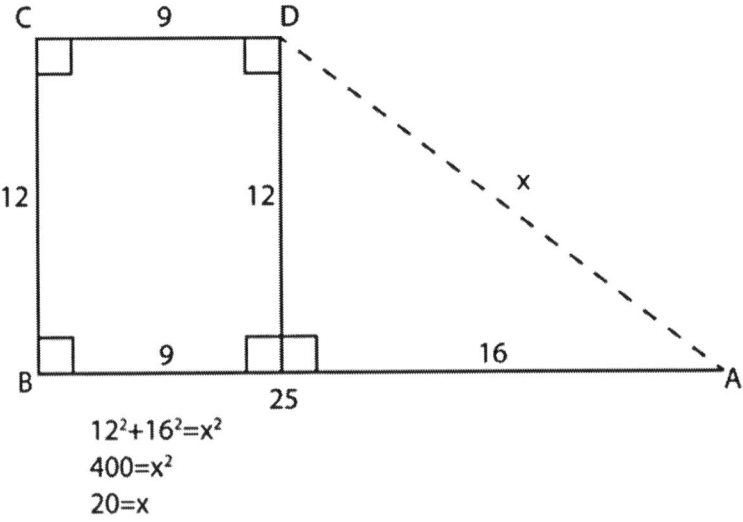

$$12^2+16^2=x^2$$
$$400=x^2$$
$$20=x$$

Your diagram leads you to a simple right- triangle solution!

Summary for the Catalyst Technique

To improve your accuracy on SAT Math questions, be sure to:

- Take your time!

- Resist the urge to solve SAT math questions "in your head."

- Practice the *Catalyst Technique* on all your review questions and carry that process forward to your timed tests and then to your SAT.

- Remember that the questions in SAT math sections are arranged in order of difficulty. As Catalysts 3,4, and 5 suggest, you may need to perform several steps in order to solve the medium/difficult questions.

REVIEW FOR SENTENCE COMPLETION
POE helps you solve SAT questions as it helped Sherlock Holmes solve cases

Most of the standard SAT textbooks discuss "Process of Elimination," or POE. This simply means that you cross-out obviously wrong answers in order arrive at the solution.

Here's how to use POE on the sentence completion sections of the SAT.

This **EXAMPLE** appears on Page 99 of *Barron's*.

> Known for his commitment to numerous worthy causes, the philanthropist deserved
>
> _____ for his _____.

Your first step is to write *simple* words into the blanks. Read the sentence quickly, then re-read it very, very slowly. As you whisper it to yourself, look for clues that will enable you to find a basic word that fits into the sentence.

Examples of basic words would be up/down, good/bad, right/wrong, dull/sharp, help/hurt, praise/blame, generous/stingy. *The simpler the better.*

Then, *use your pencil to write your simple words into the test booklet.*

Since the person described in the sentence is helping worthy causes, you could write something like **praise** into the first blank and **help** into the second blank. You don't even have to know the meaning of philanthropist in order to fill-in the blanks. The phrase "worthy causes" is enough of a clue to get you going.

After you've written-in your basic words, you go to the solutions lettered A-E. **X-out incorrect answers** and **underline** possibly correct answers.

A.   recognition…folly Cross-out **A** because folly does not mean help

B.   blame…hypocrisy Cross-out **B** because blame does not mean praise

C.   reward…modesty Underline **C** as possibly correct

D.   admonishment…wastefulness Cross out **D** because wastefulness does not mean help

E.   credit…altruism Underline **E.** This works because both answers seem to match the basic words written into the blanks.

You are left with possible answers: C and E. Which is better?

Go back to **C**. Would someone who "gave to worthy causes" expect to receive a reward? No. Therefore, cross out **C**.

That leaves just one remaining answer, E, which is correct!

Be sure to write your simple word solutions into the blanks. If you try to solve these SAT questions "in your head," you may become confused or waste time. It's easier and quicker to work when you have a reference point upon which to focus.

By writing your simple word solutions into the test book, you are putting less stress on your mind because the words are right in front of you. You don't have to remember those simple words and simultaneously figure-out the solution. You've relieved your mind of an extra job and can dedicate all your energy toward finding the answer.

As you use POE to eliminate incorrect answers, put a big **X** over an answer that you know (or strongly suspect) is wrong and put a light underline ____ under a solution that might be correct.

The **X's** and ____'s are your guideposts. ***Once you've X-ed out a solution, you don't have to waste time wondering about that answer choice.***

Then, once you've gone through letters A through E, if you have 4 X's and one ____, your answer choice is clear !

If you have 3 marked with an **X** and 2 underlined, forget about those **X's** and focus on the 2 ____, as we did, above. Look for further clues in the sentence and then use your best judgment to select your answer between the two remaining choices.

As Sherlock Holmes said to Dr. Watson, ***"When you have eliminated the impossible, whatever remains, however improbable, must be the solution."*** Even the great detective used POE!

Here's one final observation. As you improve your vocab by practicing with the cards, you will find rewards in three sections of the SAT: your essay, your critical reading, and your sentence completion. Building vocab really pays off—here on the SAT, and later in college. So, keep plugging away at that vocab list!

REVIEW FOR CRITICAL READING
Technique 1: Inverse the Curse

Imagine this. It's SAT Saturday, and if you're like most of us, you are tense. The pressure's on! You open your test booklet and start a critical reading section of the SAT, hoping beyond hope that the passage is something that you *like*.

But, of course, it's not something that you like. It's something that you dislike, that you loathe, that you despise, ***that you detest***! And you're trapped in this hot classroom, reading about tectonic plates that move under San Francisco, prompting earthquake warnings. Or, about undersea volcanoes whose eruptions formed the Hawaiian Islands.

These are the kinds of topics that I dislike: tectonic plates, earthquakes, and volcanoes. And, these are the subjects that constantly appeared and re-appeared on my SAT. Did the test writers in Princeton, New Jersey, know that I detested these reading passages? Is that why they included them on the tests that I took? Was someone in Jersey trying to torture me?

Or, was there something else happening here that I needed to understand so that I could overcome my SAT critical-reading anxiety issue?

When I was motivated to improve my critical reading score, I developed a technique I call **Inverse the Curse**. This tactic helped to improve my critical reading score, and it can help improve yours, too! It's named after the *Reverse the Curse* ice cream flavor that Brigham's created in 2004 to break the "Curse of the Bambino."

You baseball fans might know that the Boston Red Sox did not win a championship from 1918, when they traded Babe Ruth to the Yankees, until the 2004 season, the year that Brigham's created the *Reverse the Curse* ice cream. According to baseball lore, trading Babe Ruth, nicknamed "The Bambino," cursed the Red Sox and helped their dreaded Yankee rivals win all those World Series championships.

 Brigham's Ice Cream, based in Boston, hoped that the new ice cream flavor would undo the "Curse of the Bambino" and turn things around for the Red Sox.

It worked! The Red Sox went on to win the World Series in 2004. The "Curse of the Bambino" was broken! To celebrate the victory, Brigham's re-named the ice cream *The Curse Reversed*.

How does all this talk about curses and ice cream relate to the SAT? For me, the critical reading section of the SAT was my *curse*. And, to be admitted into the school I wanted to attend, I needed to raise my critical reading score. *I had to reverse the SAT critical-reading curse*.

I thought about my previous SAT experiences. What was holding me back from reaching the score I knew I could achieve? I went to the indoor pool, hoping for an inspiration. As I lapped back and forth, the answer came to me: I was re-acting to the critical reading topics that I detested by getting so worked-up that I lost my focus. Once I was in this reactive state, I was doomed.

The solution? I simply had to control my non-productive reactions.

To be effective, I had to inverse the reading passage's curse and convince myself that the topic was something that I really, really liked. That way, instead of hating the reading passage and wasting time fuming about the SAT and the loathsome subject I was reading, I could **maintain my focus** and forge ahead.

Here's how I trained myself to *inverse the curse*. I deliberately read editorials, stories, and articles that were not my favorites. And, instead of despising them, I said to myself: "This is really interesting. I can't think of anything else in the entire world that I would rather be reading."

For you *Star Wars* fans, this mental attitude is what Luke Skywalker calls the "Jedi Mind Trick."

Call it what you want. It worked. By memorizing vocab and using the *Inverse the Curse* technique, my critical reading score rose by 130 points. Having experienced this kind of success is one reason that I teach SAT prep. If these techniques worked for me, they can work for you!

Visualize that it's SAT Saturday and that you're starting a critical reading passage whose subject is "How tectonic plate movement caused the San Francisco earthquake." Instead of despising the passage—your instinctive reaction—you inverse the curse and say to yourself, "There's nothing else I'd rather be doing now than reading this."

Now, you're on your way to making life a lot easier for yourself. You've defused your tense reaction and dissolved your non-productive anxiety. As a result, your focus will improve, and so will your accuracy. You will avoid wasting time and energy hating the reading passage. By inversing the curse, you will be able to direct your attention toward your work, taking it one question at a time in a calm and controlled manner.

From my own test taking experiences and from watching my students working on practice tests, I have come to realize how much time and mental effort is wasted on hating the SAT. ***This emotional reaction disrupts your focus and affects your score.*** Practice the *Inverse the Curse* technique during your SAT prep and you will discover that your anxiety level will drop and that ability to focus will increase.

Let's move on to a couple of other techniques you can use on the SAT critical reading sections.

Technique 2: Reduce eye strain and save time by using both hands and making reference marks

Since the SAT session can take almost five hours, it's helpful to bring a snack and something to drink to maintain your energy level throughout the test. It's also important to ***reduce eye strain*** caused by your having to shift focus from the questions to the text and back to the questions.

Excessive eye strain can create pain and cause you to lose focus. And, by now, you know that losing focus can cost you points. To minimize eye strain, practice using both your hands during your SAT prep. Here's how.

Imagine that you are reading Question 1 that refers to Line 7 in the reading passage. If you are right-handed, like me, you're holding your pencil in your right hand. ***Keep that pencil pointed to Question 1***.

Then, ***place your left index finger right on Line 7 of the reading passage.*** As you are working on your answer, you will have to shift your focus from Question 1 back to Line 7. Your eyes will be moving back and forth between those two spots.

If you *anchor* those two spots, you won't have to find them over and over again. Having to re-locate Question 1 or Line 7 over and over will waste precious seconds and will stress your eye muscles.

If you are left-handed, reverse these hand directions: hold your pencil in your left hand and point it to Question 1; place your right index finger on Line 7.

You can also *mark* a specific section of the passage with an **X**, or an *underline*, or a *slash*— anything that your eye can use as a **reference point**. Your goal is to avoid having to find those key spots over and over as you strive to answer the questions.

Practice using both hands and making reference marks in your test booklet as you work on your review questions and timed tests.

Technique 3: Spend more time on the questions. Solve "specific" questions first

You have prepared yourself to inverse the curse, to trick yourself into thinking that the reading passage is interesting even though you may detest it.

You've also practiced using reference points in order to save time, reduce eye strain, and improve accuracy. What's next?

1. *Quickly read the passage.* Skim-read it. Get a general sense of what it's about: history, literature, science, etc. You're doing a scan, a quick overview.

2. *Then, go to the questions.* You will see questions that refer to specific words, lines, or paragraphs. Let's call these *specific* questions. And, you will see questions that relate to the "topic as a whole," which we'll label as *general* questions.

3. *Circle the specific questions and answer them first.*

Why should you answer the specific ones first? For two reasons: since the specific questions *direct you to the exact section of the passage*, you will not have to search for the location. The question *directs you to the spot* where you will find the answer. It's like an *open book test* with questions that tell you where to find the answers.

The questions that refer to the "passage as a whole" generally require an understanding of the entire reading passage. They will take more time for you to answer. Plus, if you answer all the specific questions first, you will have a better knowledge of the entire passage! That will make it easier for you to answer the general questions.

How to Develop an Edge for
Critical Reading Questions

An "edge" is something that gives you an advantage. For the critical reading section of the SAT, you will have an edge if you do the following:

- Maintain your focus even though you really detest the topic of the reading passage. *Inverse the Curse*!

- Skim-read the passage.

- Read the questions and circle the numbers of those questions that refer to specific lines or paragraphs.

- Using both hands and reference marks as guides, answer specific questions first, answer general questions last.

- Think of the critical reading section as an open book test. You don't have to know the answers beforehand. Your job is to find the answers right in front of you, in the reading passage.

- Use POE to eliminate incorrect answer choices, just as we reviewed in the previous chapter.

REVIEW FOR WRITING SKILLS AND THE ESSAY
The schedule will navigate you through key review topics

By working just a few minutes every day, you will make it through the material you need to know for the writing skills section of the SAT. The schedule will direct you to specific pages in *Barron's* that contain key review topics, including:

- A review of grammar and usage

- How to improve sentences and paragraphs

- How to structure your essay

As you progress through these topics, make cards for any grammatical facts that need further study. Proceed the same way as you are doing for your math and vocab cards: write the topic on the blank side of the card, then describe and illustrate the concept on the lined side. Here are a couple of my own writing skills cards:

Compound Subjects joined by or/nor

When a subject consists of a singular and plural noun joined by either/or, or neither/nor, the number of the verb is determined by the closer subject.

Example: Either the two small oranges or the huge *grapefruit is* capable of providing enough Vitamin C.

Example rephrased: Either the huge grapefruit or the two small *oranges are* capable of providing enough Vitamin C.

You may find multiple choice writing skills questions that involve the grammatical concept of an "inserted expression." Here's an example: The player who I think is the best is named MJ.

The phrase *I think* is the ***inserted expression***. How does it affect the pronoun before it? Should the pronoun be who (subjective) or whom (objective)?

Here's the rule for inserted expressions, a concept for which I need constant reinforcement. My card looks like this.

Inserted Expressions

Inserted Expressions (such as *I think* and *I know*) should be ignored when you determine case.

Ex: The player **who** *I think* **is the best** is named Michael.

The phrase *I think* is the inserted expression. The pronoun who remains in the nominative case, not affected by the inserted expression.

Ex: The player **to whom** *I know* **the award will be given** is named Michael.

In this example, the inserted expression *I know* does not change the objective case of the pronoun *whom*.

Here are a few other grammatical concepts that are on my students' hit list:

- The subject of an infinitive is in the ***objective*** case.

  Example 1: They expect ***me*** to bake the bread.
  Example 2: They expect ***John and me*** to bake the bread.

  Beware: You may be tempted to use "I" instead of ***me*** in Example 2. To reinforce the need for the objective case (me), re-read Example 2 without the words *John and*. Then, your ear will tell you that ***me*** is the correct choice.

- The subject of a gerund is in the ***possessive*** case.

  Example: Do you agree with ***his*** attempting to drive through downtown Boston during rush hour?

- ***that*** versus ***which***

  that = restrictive: no comma
  Example: The recipe that was voted the most delectable contains all natural ingredients.

  which = non-restrictive: use commas
  Example: The recipe, which is featured in the current issue of *Gourmet* magazine, contains all natural ingredients.

- ***Redundant*** words and phrases. Here are some *redundancies* followed by their corrections:

  general consensus   This should be stated simply as "consensus." Since consensus means "general opinion," you do not need to include the word *general,* which is the redundancy.

  at the present time = now, currently, presently
  I *personally* think = I think, I believe
  in my *personal* opinion = in my opinion

- ***Parallelism*** Watch for violations in parallelism, especially when you use phrases like "neither...nor" and "either...or." Example: He decided neither ***to drive*** to the movies nor ***did he want to walk to*** Starbucks. To maintain parallelism, rewrite as "He decided neither ***to go*** to the movies nor ***to walk*** to Starbucks." Be sure that the words that follow *neither* and *nor* are expressed ***exactly*** in the same way- in this case, the infinitives *to go* and *to walk.*

- ***Shifting person or tense*** Example: If ***one*** decides to cook an elaborate dinner, ***you*** must be sure to have all the ingredients on hand. Shifting from *one* to *you* violates parallelism. Solution: keep both pronouns the same. If ***you*** decide to cook an elaborate dinner, ***you*** must be sure to have all the ingredients on hand.

Barron's includes an assortment of practice questions designed to reinforce key grammar concepts. I suggest that you work on one practice question at a time. Use POE to eliminate obviously incorrect answers, and immediately check your answer against the solutions that *Barron's* provides. If there's a grammatical construction or topic that trips you up, make an index card for it and add it to your "unfamiliar" stack for further study.

Your Grammar and Vocab Review Will Bolster Your Essay
Precise Grammar + Sparkling Vocab + Exciting Themes = Essay Success

It's obvious, isn't it, that as you refine your grammar and bolster your vocab, you will also be prepping for the essay writing assignment of the SAT! Precise grammar, sharp vocab, and vivid examples from your theme cards all contribute to your ability to succeed on this section of the test.

As you create your theme cards, may I suggest that you include and memorize details such as names, dates, and events. You can do it! Think of how you can recite sports facts, how you can remember keystrokes for your smartphone, and how you can recall the lyrics of your favorite songs. Use any memory trick you can to memorize the details on your theme cards. These details will come in handy when you tackle the essay assignment.

It's important to select essay themes that interest you, rather than themes that you *think* the graders will like. You'll have more fun creating and memorizing your theme cards when you focus on topics that are important to *you*. When you're working on your SAT, your enthusiasm for your topics will carry through into your writing. As a result, you will earn points for including apt examples and insights that support and enhance your point of view.

In class, I distribute theme card topics that I think are exciting. The class senses my excitement, which focuses their attention and starts them thinking about topics that are important to them. Here's the Rembrandt/Matisse theme cards, followed by the questions and connections that they provoke for me.

Rembrandt	vs.	Matisse
self-portrait 1634		Portrait Madame Matisse 1903

Rembrandt 1606-1669
Dutch "old master"
Style=representational
Detailed, three-dimensional
Full tonal range from deep shadows
to bright highlights
Color not vivid=muted
Classical composition

Matisse- 1869-1954
French-Fauvist School
In French, "fauve" means "wild beast"

Considered savage by the art world
Shocking use of color was not initially embraced
because it was not realistic
Said "Exactitude is not truth."
Sought to create emotion through vivid use of
color. Very bright lighting. Now recognized as a
leading figure in history of art.

The first connections that I made after reading these cards were a series of questions:

- What is it about the visual arts that has drawn us to museums from one century to another?

- Does a visual work have to be "representational" for it to be considered "art"?

- How could two artists- both passionate, both skilled, and both using the same materials- create portraits that are so different?

I then recall the Matisse's quote "Exactitude is not truth." Here's my train of thought- the connections- that this quote provokes in me. To Matisse, the essence of his subject was not in how it simply appeared to the eye. Its essence was more subtle, not necessarily so obvious as mere physical appearance. The purpose of art, Matisse believed, was to ***reveal a deeper truth*** via a visual vocabulary that often deviated from mere representation.

My mind skips to another concept. I think about how people behave. Do you always verbalize ***everything*** that you are thinking? Do your words, alone, accurately convey your complete thought? Or, are there subtleties in tone or expression that accompany your words that also relay information about what you think? Sometimes, the way words are conveyed and the accompanying facial expressions may actually contain more truth than the words themselves!

Forensic detectives make a living attempting to determine the "truth behind the words." Inter-relate the mind of the detective to the mind of Matisse: what a detective attempts to deduce about a suspect is similar to what Matisse attempts to portray about his subject: the "truth," the inner essence that may be hidden by the obvious outer appearance. Matisse believed that his bold, simplified forms and vivid colors revealed more of the subject's essence than a precise depiction could ever render.

Then, I wonder, "Why did some of Matisse's contemporaries despise the very works that today are revered and sell for millions of dollars? Were Matisse's critics stuck in some rigid notion of what constituted art, and thus unable to appreciate Matisse's use of color and form? Can this inability to 'see' another point of view affect scientists or political leaders, today? Can this kind of mental blindness affect you and me?"

The connections you make about your theme cards can inspire you as you compose your essay. That's why I've expanded the Matisse/Rembrandt cards here, just as I do in the live SAT prep class: to point-out that it's important to think about your themes from different angles and to be ready to relate your connections to the SAT. Understand and appreciate that your cards and "connections" may differ from mine and from those of your classmates. That's how it should be. After all, we are not all the same and our minds don't work exactly alike!

Go for relevance, think about what your topics mean in the largest possible context. Glean the wisdom from your theme cards so that your prep work illumines and inspires (rather than bores) *you*!

Speaking of relevance: consider the Churchill card. How relevant is that! Let's explore how its topic relates to us, right now. Every day, the news services relay details about a variety international crises that vary in form and location but that never seem to disappear. Will diplomacy *always* be able to resolve these on-going international crises? Or, will our leaders sometimes have to resort to a military solution?

Churchill, on Appeasers
"An appeaser is one who feeds a crocodile hoping it will eat him last."
Winston Churchill, British Statesman

Appeasement= policy followed by Brit Prime Minister Neville Chamberlain= making concessions to Hitler to avoid military conflict<WWII 1935 to 1939 Chamberlain signed "Munich Agreement"

30 Sept 1938 permitting Nazi Germany to annex areas of Czechoslovakia called the "Sudetenland."
Churchill warned Brits + French that appeasing Hitler would not work. But Europe was war-weary and did not listen to WC. They wanted **"peace at any price."** Sept 1939 Hitler invades Poland. Brits declare war on Germany.
WC's warnings proved **correct.** Churchill becomes Prime Minister and leads England to victory in WWII.

The Churchill card illustrates that diplomacy, alone, could not stop Hitler's aggression. In this instance, the correct response to Hitler's aggression was military. Does this paradigm always work? What about Korea, Vietnam, Iraq, Afghanistan- what was the correct response then? Was America's military action correct in **all** of these situations? Or, should we have used diplomacy, collaborated with the United Nations, or instituted economic sanctions instead of risking the lives of the men and women in our armed forces?

This topic so intrigued one of my college professors that he created a course at Harvard which he titled "War." Professor Hoffman's terrific lectures detailed various wars throughout history and sought to answer the question: why do men engage in warfare? Is war always the correct solution to an international crisis? Is war the result of mistakes and misunderstandings among political leaders and governments? Or, is war an irrational response, a function of a primitive aspect of our biological makeup that has outlived its usefulness but which is impossible to control or eradicate?

When I get going on this topic, my class senses my "heat" and then things get exciting. We start making associations, posing questions, making history come alive. ***The topic becomes real*** - not just a dry paragraph in a faded history book, but a critical issue that exists today, that affects the lives of our family and friends who may be deployed in combat areas right now.

My cinema theme cards also stir things up. I ask the class "When does Luke Skywalker destroy the Death Star, at the beginning or at the end of *Star Wars*? "

Of course, everyone knows it's at the conclusion.

A blockbuster film moves from conflict to conflict, from small conflicts to big conflicts. The biggest conflict occurs at the end. The climax! Talented scriptwriters build their scripts according to this paradigm, sequencing from minor conflict to major conflict to resounding climax. The reason for the buildup is that if the climax occurs at the beginning, the rest of the film would seem boring. We in the audience would walk away saying something like "the film started-out pretty good, but then it was so dull that I fell asleep as soon as I finished my popcorn."

Structure your essay, I tell the class, just as a skilled screenwriter designs a screenplay. For the SAT, I suggest that you have an introduction, a conclusion, and ***three middle paragraphs*** that relay *three distinct examples* to support your point of view. Connect your paragraphs so that your essay flows from one paragraph to the next, just as a successful film flows from one sequence to the next. Insert your **strongest point in the third paragraph**. Then, your essay will go out with a bang, just as do films like *Star Wars*, *Jaws*, and *Titanic*! Compose your assignment using this paradigm, and The Force (and likely a nice score) will be with you!

How to Find Topics for Your Theme Cards
Here's my stack for the next Prep Class

It's easy to find topics for your theme cards. When you come across a topic that *you like,* bookmark it. If you find an interesting article in a newspaper or magazine, copy it; if it's a story on the net, print it; if it's a topic you discuss at school, make a note of its source. Make a stack of these topics, and then choose your favorite ones to use as theme cards.

Here's my stack of new topics I've collected for the next SAT prep class:

- "The Right Answer is 'No': It may be uncomfortable, especially for people pleasers; Ways to master the art." By Elizabeth Bernstein, from the Wall Street Journal, 03/11/2014. Section D, Page 1.

- "Commander William McRaven relays ten lessons from basic SEAL training at University of Texas commencement." McRaven stressed the importance of making your bed every morning, taking on obstacles headfirst, and realizing that it's OK to be a "sugar cookie." From the net on May 20, 2014.

- "Walmart's 'Made-in-USA' push exposes strains of manufacturing rebirth in the United States." Since much of America's manufacturing has been outsourced to other countries, "a lot of the tribal knowledge and skill sets are gone because the humans who used to do that work in America have either retired or died." From the net on June 04, 2014. PS What are the implications of this article?

- "Fat (reconsidered): Americans have been told for decades to avoid red meat, butter, cheese, and other fatty foods because they cause heart disease. But, do they really? The dubious science behind the anti-fat crusade." By Nina Teicholz, from the *Wall Street Journal,* 05/03/2014. Section C, Page 1.

- From Daniel Goleman's terrific book, *Emotional Intelligence* Page 90-92 "Flow: The Neurobiology of Excellence... experienced by hundreds of diverse men and women- rock climbers, chess champions, surgeons, basketball players, engineers, managers, even filing clerks. The state they describe is called "flow" by Mihaly Csikszentmihalyi, the University of Chicago psychologist who has collected such accounts of peak performance during two decades of research. Athletes know this state of grace as "the zone," where excellence becomes effortless, crowd and competitors disappearing into a blissful steady absorption in the moment....In flow, the emotions are not just contained and channeled, but positive, energized, and aligned with the task at hand. To be caught in the ennui of depression or the agitation of anxiety is to be barred from flow..."

You can see that the topics and sources are varied. The common thread among them is that they captured my attention. Proceed in the same way and, in a couple of weeks, you'll have a stack of varied themes that interest you. ***Create your theme cards from the ones you like the most!*** As a result, you will be able to infuse your essay with credibility, clarity and coherence, attributes of good writing that will score points for you on the SAT.

To sum up *Review for the Essay:* create theme cards on topics that interest you; include and memorize data points on your cards; think about what the cards mean, making connections and asking yourself how the themes relate to you and to the world. Each fact, each detail, each connection you make is yet another data point you'll have available to cite on your SAT!

PART FOUR:
FOCUS AND PACING-TIMED TESTS

YOUR FINAL STEP: TIMED TESTS
Congratulations. You are almost ready to do battle with the SAT

If you have followed our prep schedule, you're way ahead of the average SAT test-taker. Think of all the work you've already done, and imagine the tension building in other students who haven't put in the time and effort that you have expended over the past few weeks.

Your SAT prep rewards you in many ways: you are calmer because you are doing something positive; you are prepared because you have done your memory and review work; you feel better about yourself because, deep down, you know that you're giving the SAT your best shot.

So, pat yourself on the back. Treat yourself to a smoothie or a latte...*and work on those index cards between sips.* Remember that your memory work continues right up to SAT Saturday. If you're like most of my students and me, you still have some math, vocab, and theme cards to commit to memory over the next couple of weeks. Keep that memory process going even as you enter the last step of your SAT Prep.

This final phase of your prep involves the clock. You will find 5 practice SAT's at the back of *Barron's*. Complete any two of these practice tests. As you do so, follow these guidelines:

- Use pencil on all practice tests.
- Use the same calculator that you will bring to the SAT.
- Work on one section at a time with a clock in front of you so that you get used to SAT timing.
- Read all the instructions that appear in the boxes so that you become super-familiar with the SAT's format.
- Go for accuracy, not for speed.
- When time is up, check your answers against those provided in the "Answers Explained" section that follows each practice test.

Be sure to read the entire chapter of this book before you begin your timed tests. You'll find helpful tactics here that are designed to reduce anxiety, save time, and improve your accuracy... the on-going mission of this book! Let's start with the technique I call *Maria's Focus Booster.*

MARIA'S FOCUS BOOSTER
Helps you to ignore irritating distractions

My piano teacher, Maria, used a technique to prep her students for their recitals at the Boston Conservatory. I call the tactic *Maria's Focus Booster* because it's designed to help you maintain your concentration during even the most annoying disturbances you could imagine.

Here's what Maria did. She would invite about thirty of her piano students to attend dress rehearsal a few days before a scheduled concert. The performer, usually a junior or senior piano major, would begin playing. As the pianist approached a very difficult section of the composition, Maria would stand up, scraping her metal chair against the wooden floor.

Clomping toward the bookcase in her high heels, Maria would take hold of a huge hardcover book, lift it up to chin level, and let it go. WOMP! I couldn't believe that any performer would be able to maintain focus during this fracas. But, she did!

Maria would then escalate her noise making. She would walk to the heavy wooden double-doors at the back of the room, open one of them, and then slam it shut. The loud BOOM would make us jump! But the performer, undisturbed, continued playing.

The final disturbance was the worst. Walking behind the performer, Maria would approach the fifth-floor windows that looked out toward Fenway Park. She would move one of the curtains and, with her arm already lifted, would karate-chop the venetian blind. How could anyone forget that sharp, scraping screech!

After attending my first dress rehearsal, I asked the performer how she maintained her concentration. "We're used to playing through the noise," she said.

"Maria does this all the time, and it helps us to deal with all the sounds that occur during the concert. You know, people coughing, moving their chairs, and talking during the performance. If we can deal with Maria's noise, we can deal with theirs."

Since I still remember *Maria's Focus Booster* in such detail, I decided to use the technique in my SAT prep classes. My goal is the same as Maria's: to fortify my students' ability to overcome the various distractions that arise on SAT Saturday.

If you have taken a test like the SAT, you might recall disturbances such as:

- noisy test takers
- annoying proctors
- ticking clocks
- squeaky chairs
- clanking radiators
- irritating sounds from outside the classroom

To overcome these annoyances, practice *Maria's Focus Booster*. Get together with a couple of your friends and have one of them play the role of Maria while the others work on SAT timed tests. See if you can maintain your focus during the distractions.

If you train yourself to expect such annoyances during the test, then you'll be able to deal with them and to stay on course.

Test takers who are surprised by the disturbances—or who resent them—will likely be victimized by them. ***You who expect the disturbances to occur and who are prepared for them are less likely to re-act to these distractions and more able to maintain your focus.***

And, as you know by now, your success on the SAT depends upon maintaining your focus while others may not! That's your edge: your ability to ignore the distractions and to focus on the test, taking it one question at a time. Practice *Maria's Focus Booster* with your classmates and you will be helping each other achieve your common goal: to do your personal best on the SAT.

TIMED TESTS: THE ESSAY

How to Improve Your Essay's Appeal
Write for the Mind, the Eye, and the Ear

Barron's and the other standard SAT textbooks suggest how to structure your essay: introductory paragraph, two or three middle paragraphs to develop your point of view, and a strong concluding paragraph. I'll relay some further suggestions designed to improve your essay's creativity and appeal... suggestions that complement the excellent techniques you will find in Chapter 7 of *Barron's*.

First and foremost: ***A clear essay is easy for the graders to read!***

When I pick up one of my student's essays, the first thing I notice is the handwriting. If I see scrawl like this, my heart rate immediately...

... accelerates and my head begins to pound and I start to wonder why I have to read this essay and if I should take a break and maybe need of to Starbucks for a very, very strong cup of coffee in order to boost my energy and that will help me to stay awake for at least another hour so that I can get the most of these essay grades and...

Can you imagine how it feels to read ten essays with handwriting like this? Definitely not fun. So, if you want to get on the good side of your grader, make your writing as neat as you can. You can print or write in longhand… whichever you do better. Use a Number 2 pencil and compose your essay with enough intensity so that it scans clearly.

My scrawl is also an example of a *run-on sentence*. I see plenty of these monsters in my students' essays. Run-on's are difficult to understand. They're so long that the reader loses focus. Plus, they look and sound "wrong." Writing not only affects your intellect; it also touches your eyes and ears.

So, beware of long sentences and huge, blocky paragraphs that confuse the mind and the senses. Like run-on sentences, these super-sized paragraphs are very difficult to read. The solution: **break-up huge paragraphs into smaller ones** and aim for that 4-5 paragraph structure that *Barron's* suggests.

In addition to sloppy penmanship and run-on's, another common essay fault is the lack of interesting background material. Over the years, I have read countless essays that reference the *The Big Five:* Washington, Lincoln, Kennedy, King and whoever is the current President. It's rare for me to read two essays in a row without coming across mention of at least one of *The Big Five.*

If reference to these icons is compelling, then go for it. But, test-takers who lack background material will often rely on information that has been drilled into their minds over and over. That's why my daughter Ann cited Catholic dogma as her tension level rose during the SAT essay. And I think that's why many students rely on *The Big Five:* it's what they manage to remember during the stress that accompanies the SAT.

There are a couple of disadvantages to your citing frequently used background material. When grading essays, I become bored by the constant mention of *The Big Five*. I yearn to read something new and different. Furthermore, some of the references to *The Big Five* seem forced. After all, even *The Big Five* cannot possibly be relevant background material for every SAT essay assignment.

It's hard to stand-out from the pack if your references are similar to those of many other test takers. That's why I encourage you to create and memorize a wide variety of theme cards. You already know about *The Big Five*. Gather other interesting background material to embellish your essay. Set yourself apart from the crowd when you compose your SAT essay. ***Include apt and unusual details that prompt the graders to say to themselves, "Wow, this is really interesting work!"***

Oops! The Erase and Rewrite Trap

As you prepare to do a timed SAT essay, beware of the ***Erase and Rewrite Trap***. Here's how this frustrating process unfolds.

You're excited as you start the SAT, which is often with the essay assignment. You begin writing, full of energy, wanting to get off to a good start on the test. After a few minutes of writing, though, you lose faith in your composition and wonder if you should re-start your essay with a different point of view.

As you become more anxious, you react to a tense inner voice that grows louder and louder, proclaiming, "This isn't the right answer. This isn't what the graders want."

Once you succumb to this inner critic, you erase your essay and start over with a different viewpoint that you think is "right" and which will please the graders. By now, you may have consumed 7 of the 25 minutes allotted for your essay. That leaves you only 18 minutes for your re-write.

The *Erase and Rewrite Trap* puts pressure on you. Unproductive pressure! What's the solution? Learn to manage your self-critical inner voice of doubt by practicing the following suggestions during your timed essays.

First, read the essay assignment and the instructions very slowly. Whisper them to yourself. You know what I mean: **read the instructions just as you would sing a song to yourself** without actually vocalizing the tune aloud. As you are listening to yourself read the topic, make some connections. Using your theme cards as background material, jot down concepts from them that relate to the assignment – personalities, quotes, historical facts, scientific inventions, etc.

Remind yourself that your job is to create a coherent essay that illustrates your point of view. You can be *pro* (in agreement), *con* (in disagreement), or *qualify* (sometimes pro, sometimes con). Use data from your theme cards to support your viewpoint. *During your practice tests, keep your theme cards nearby and refer to them as you are planning and writing your essay.* By doing so, you will reinforce the various topics that you've amassed on the cards, further preparing yourself for the real SAT.

Some test takers think that there is only one correct point of view. This is not true. The SAT essay assignments are general in nature and allow for many points of view. When my daughter Christine proofread this section last night, she confessed that she started her SAT essay three times. Wow! If you have a vivid imagination like Christine, you could probably imagine several different points of view for the essay assignment.

You only have time for one point of view, though. ***Spend the first 5 minutes deciding upon which point of view you can best support***. Jot down relevant themes and concepts from your theme cards, studies, experiences, and observations.

For which viewpoint do you have the best background material? Which point of view can you relay with the best clarity? For which viewpoint do you have the best inner conviction? As you make your decision, ***disregard any inner voice that attempts to deduce what viewpoint the graders want***.

How could you ever really know the mind of your graders, anyway? You have never met them. You don't know who they are. You will never, ever be able to predict if your graders are "pro" or "con," if they are Democrats or Republicans, musicians or ice skaters, New Yorkers or Los Angelenos, jocks or scientists…or both! Don't even waste a second of your precious time trying to deduce the graders' identities, desires, or personalities.

Cut to the essentials. The graders' job is to assess your writing skills. They will be awarding points for coherence, originality, flow, grammar, etc. Your job is to decide upon a point of view and then to express it as coherently and convincingly as possible. That's how you will be graded. ***Once you decide upon a point of view…pro, con, or qualify… go for it!***

As I tell my students, when you write the essay, you are the loudspeaker. You're the ***voice that proclaims*** what you think.

The essay writing process is the opposite of the critical reading sections in which you are the ***ear that listens*** to what someone else thinks.

So, make you voice as loud and as clear as you can. That's what writing is about: relaying your concepts with clarity and creativity. Dismiss the inner doubt that wonders, "Is this is what the graders want?" and replace it with strong writing that proclaims, "***This is what I believe, and here's why***."

TIMED TESTS: MATH

Math questions sequence Easy-Medium-Hard. But all count the same toward your score!

Math questions on the SAT are arranged in order of difficulty. For example, a math section with 20 multiple-choice questions will be set-up as follows: the first third of the questions are the easiest (Q 1-6); the middle third are medium difficulty (Q7-14); and the final third (Q 15-20) are the most difficult.

Since all questions count the same toward your score, focus on the easy & medium questions before you tackle the difficult ones.

There will also be a math section that contains both multiple choice and grid-in questions. The easy-medium-difficult pattern is the same—with one twist.

Let's say that an 18-question math section contains 8 multiple choice and 10 grid-in questions.

The easy-medium-difficult pattern will apply to the multiple choice questions: the first three will be easy (Q1-3); the next three will be medium (Q4-6), and the final two will be difficult (Q7-8).

Then, the ***pattern starts all over again*** for the grid in questions: Q9-11 are easy; Q12-16 medium; Q17-18 difficult.

When you are working on one of those 18-question math sections that contain both multiple choice and grid-in's, first tackle the easy & medium multiple choice (Q1-6)…skip the difficult ones (Q7- 8)… and work on the easy & medium grid-in's. If you have time, go back to the difficult multiple choice and difficult grid-in's.

As time winds down on a math section, if you have to choose between (a) checking your work on two or three of the easy/medium questions or (b) answering one difficult question, go for choice (a). You'll probably have a better chance of answering those easy-medium questions than trying to tackle a difficult question with time winding down.

When you are working on both practice tests and on the actual SAT, you will find that your solutions come more quickly for the first few questions. But, as you work further into the medium questions, you will have to spend more time on them. That's normal. Remember, you may have to set-up two formulas or diagrams to solve medium and difficult questions, as we discussed in the Review section of this book titled the *Catalyst Approach.*

Summary of Suggestions for Math Timed Tests

- Use the **Catalyst Approach** to match easy questions with Catalysts 1 and 2, medium questions with Catalysts 2-3-4, and difficult questions with Catalysts 4 and 5.

- *Get your pencil moving*: write the necessary formulas into your test booklet, fill-in data, and draw diagrams. By clearly jotting down your solution steps, you will find it easier to review and to check your answers.

- Take your time. *Go for accuracy*…not for speed!

- Since all correct answers count the same toward your score, nail the easy/medium questions before spending a lot of time on the difficult ones.

TIMED TESTS: SENTENCE COMPLETION
POE a key technique for Sentence Completions
Vocab Memory also will aid you here

Sentence completion sections of the SAT follow the easy-medium-difficult pattern, similar to the same progression in which math questions are arranged. As you move forward in your sentence completion questions, you will encounter more complex sentences and more advanced vocabulary. That's why your vocab memory work will pay dividends here: you'll recognize more words and be able to eliminate obviously wrong answer choices using POE.

The chapter titled "Review for Sentence Completion" contains most of my helpful hints that relate to this part of the SAT. Refer back to that chapter, especially if you need to review the importance of POE to solve these questions.

Sample Question from Test 1 in Barron's

"It is said that the custom of shaking hands originated when primitive men held out empty hands to indicate that they had no _____ weapons and were thus _____ disposed."

Fill-in the blanks with two simple words that make sense. I chose *hidden* and *friendly*…. no *hidden* weapons and thus were *friendly* disposed.

Then, using POE, **X**-out the incorrect answer choices and **underline** the possibly-correct answers.

A. lethal..clearly **X** because clearly does not equal friendly

B. concealed..amicably **underline** letter B…possible answer

C. hidden..harmfully **X** because harmfully is not friendly

D. murderous..ill **X** because ill does not equal friendly

E. secret…finally **X** because finally is not friendly

Note that POE has eliminated four incorrect answers. The only answer choice not X'ed is letter B, which is the correct answer. You don't have to know the definition of "amicably" to solve this question because POE has automatically led you to the correct answer.

Summary of Tactics for Sentence Completion

- Fill-in the blanks with simple words that make sense.

- Use POE to eliminate answer choices that don't match the easy words you have written-into the blanks. **X**-out incorrect answers and **underline** possibly correct answers. Then, decide which underlined answer choice works best.

- Expect that SAT sentence completion sections will progress from easy to medium to difficult, similar to the arrangement of questions in SAT math sections.

TIMED TESTS: CRITICAL READING
Critical Reading is like an open-book test
Your job is just to find the answer

Barron's Practice Test 1 contains a reading passage about Charles Darwin. The preface identifies Darwin as "the originator of the theory of evolution." When my students read this preface, they are naturally in awe. After all, the passage is about the great Charles Darwin, the renowned scientist. But, it's also about a 26-year-old guy who's having fun in the Galapagos Islands. Here's how Lines 1-5 read:

> "Charles Darwin came to the Galapagos in 1835 on the *Beagle*; he was twenty-six. He threw the marine iguanas as far as he could into the water; he rode the tortoises and sampled their meat."

Question: This portrayal of Darwin conveys primarily a sense of his:

A.   methodical research

B.   instant commitment

C.   youthful playfulness

D.   lack of original thought

E.   steadiness of purpose

Picture a 26-year old in the tropics, throwing an iguana into the water and riding a giant turtle. Do you hear the woops as he throws the iguana into the water? Can you imagine the screams as he rides the turtle, trying to stay on its back for as long as he can? Darwin is in his own private version of Disneyland, having fun in the surf!

So, what's the correct answer?

A.   Methodical research? No way. **X**-out A.

B.   Instant commitment? Commitment to what? **X**-out B.

C.   Youthful playfulness? Could be! **Underline C.**

D.   Lack of original thought? Not even mentioned. **X**-out D.

E.   Steadiness of purpose? What purpose? **X**-out E.

Many students gravitate toward choices A, B and E because these answer choices support what they already know about Darwin: he's a great scientist. However, his greatness is not being conveyed in Lines 1 through 5. It's his youthful playfulness, Choice C, which is portrayed.

Here's the point: when you are working on critical reading questions, *let go of your preconceptions. Relieve yourself of the pressure to know the answer.* Simply read the lines in question and *find the answer.* You may not even agree with the answer. That's ok, too. Remember, when you read, you are the ear that listens.

The SAT will pose a question like this: according to the author of the passage, what aspect of Darwin's personality is being portrayed? This phrase, according to the author, means that you simply have to read those lines and discover what the author is saying. Focus on that job and that job only! Knowing that the SAT critical reading process is like an open book test should relieve some of your stress because it defines your task: *to find the answers right there in front of you.*

Summary of Tactics for Critical Reading

- ***Inverse the Curse.*** Love the reading passage!

- Use two hands and reference marks to reduce eye strain.

- Spend more time on questions.

- Answer specific questions first.

- Use POE.

- Think of the process as an open-book test.

TIMED TESTS: WRITING SKILLS MULTIPLE CHOICE QUESTIONS

Knowing the instructions beforehand will save valuable time. Make every minute count!

The Writing Skills multiple choice questions are presented to you in three sections, each with a different format:

- Improving Sentences
- Identifying Sentence Errors
- Improving Paragraphs in a Student Essay

Each of these three sections contains its own specific instructions. As you work on timed tests, read and re-read those instructions. By doing so, you will become familiar with the three formats. Then, when you take your SAT, you will not have to decipher the directions. *Your understanding the directions before SAT Saturday may save you a few valuable minutes as you work on the test.*

If there are other additional comments or directions, pay very close attention to them. Often, the SAT has a preface or other instructions in addition to the standard directions. If so, read them slowly and carefully.

Your index cards on grammar and usage will aid you as you work on the writing skills questions. This is the background material that you amassed during the Memory and Review weeks of your prep schedule. If some of your cards contain definitions or topics that still seem unfamiliar to you, continue to carry those cards with you and commit them to memory. I still had a handful of unfamiliar cards that I studied the on the way to the test center. Continue to work on your cards right to the bitter end!

Summary of Tactics for Writing Skills
Multiple Choice Questions

- Read directions for every timed test section so that you are very familiar with the three sets of instructions.

- During the SAT, pay very close attention to any additional directions or comments that are italicized or in boxes.

- To more easily spot grammar and usage errors, read the sentences very slowing, whispering them to yourself. Your ear can help guide you to the solution.

- Use POE

BEWARE THE SPEEDY TEST TAKER
Is it Speed... or Showing Off...or Something Else?

While you were still working on a test, did you ever notice that some of your classmates made a point of showing that they had already finished their exams? I remember how some of my friends would tromp to the front of the room and put their answer sheets on the teacher's desk minutes before an exam was scheduled to end.

Some would do so with theatrical flair, as if they making an onstage entrance in a Broadway play. They would drag their soles on the floor, creating an attention-getting screech. They might even click their pens and cough for added sound effects as they marched up the aisle to the front of the room.

At first, those of us who were still working on our exams felt threatened. After all, why were we struggling with the test, checking our work, making sure we had it right? Were *we* missing something?

Why did it take us so long to do the exam when other students apparently nailed it so quickly?

After a couple of grading periods, it became apparent that these speedy students were not always acing their exams. In fact, many of the students who continued to work for the entire exam sessions were getting better grades than the speedy test takers.

Once we realized this, we were not affected by the speeders. Our jealousy and doubt faded. In fact, we felt bad for them. After all, isn't the goal to achieve the best score instead of trying to beat the clock or to impress the rest of the class? And, in the long run, who really cares who finished first and who finished last?

This same kind of flashy speeder drama may occur during your SAT. Before a section of the test is over, you might notice that some students have stopped working. They may create sound effects to let everyone know that they have finished. Or, they may strike a relaxed pose, staring out the window, trying to look carefree. Right!

My suggestion to you: **do not react to the SAT speeders**. Resist the urge to rush your work because of the speeders' dramatics. Instead, work carefully and use all your allotted time working on the questions. Check your work—especially the easy/medium questions. *Give it your all for the full number of minutes and you will be rewarded in the way that really matters: a higher test score!*

What Questions Should You Review Before Time is UP?

Answer Sheet Shorthand points the way.

Here's a technique you can use on all sections of the test. It's called **Answer Sheet Shorthand**, a quick and easy way for you to tag your answers. As time is winding-down on a section of the SAT, dig-in and stay positive. Pay no attention to the speeders and focus on questions that you need to revisit.

If you **tag your answers** using **Answer Sheet Shorthand,** you can use those last few minutes to double-check the easy/medium questions and any others that you've marked for review.

Answer Sheet Shorthand suggests three tags, or marks, to identify your confidence level for each of your answers.

1. **Correct answer:** You're as sure as you can be that your answer is correct. ***Fully darken*** the bubble on the answer sheet and move forward to the next question.

2. **Probably correct:** You *lightly* bubble your answer sheet and put a slash near the question number to indicate probably correct.

    Watch the clock and allow time to check these *probably correct* questions. When a session is almost over, you go back for a final run. Rework the question, make your decision, and then fully darken that bubble on your answer sheet.

    Right after you darken your bubble, ***erase the slash*** on your answer sheet.

3. **Doubtful**—difficult question: You have no clue as to solution and cannot eliminate any incorrect answers. Lightly put a **?** near the number of the question. Work on easy/medium probably correct answers before spending a lot of time on these difficult and more time-consuming questions.

Here's how a 20-question math answer sheet might look. Slashes on Q6, 7, 15, and 17 indicate ***probably correct answers***. Question marks for Q11, 19, and 20 indicate ***doubtful*** questions. First be sure you have nailed your *probably correct* answers before you spend time on these *doubtful* ones marked with a question mark.

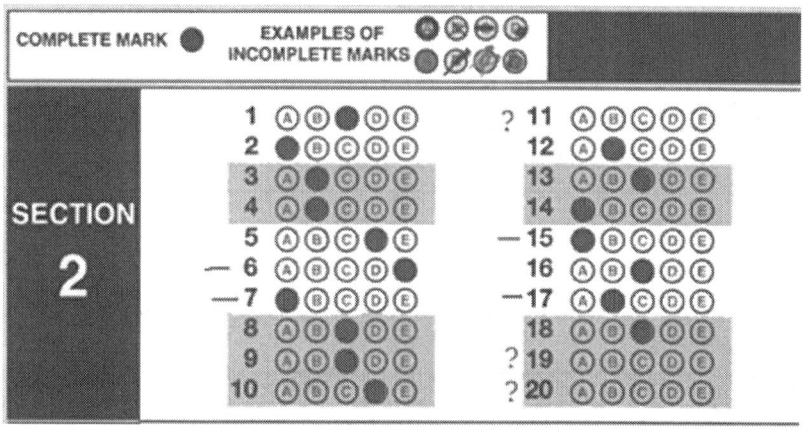

As time runs out, darken your answer bubbles and erase any remaining slashes and question marks so that you answer sheet is *clean and crisp*, as below.

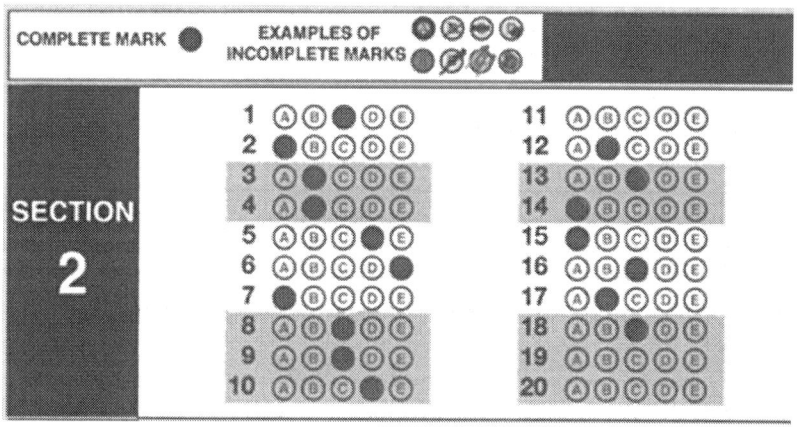

PART FIVE:
DEVELOPING YOUR SAT STRATEGY

BE YOUR STRONGEST
IN MIND, BODY, AND SPIRIT
Knowledge + Strength + Confidence = Being Prepared

Your memory work and your studies will provide you with the knowledge to help you succeed on the SAT. That's the mind aspect of your preparation, the activity most commonly associated with an SAT prep routine.

From your own life experiences, I am sure you realize that there are other key factors to consider as you prepare for the SAT. By other factors, I mean your *confidence* level (spirit) and your *stamina* (body).

Your familiarity with techniques like *Inverse the Curse, Maria's Focus Booster,* and *The Speedy Test Taker* will build your confidence level, the spirit component of your SAT prep. As you expand your knowledge base by memorizing your cards and solving practice questions, your confidence level will naturally increase. ***Mind and spirit are related: strength in mind will translate into confidence of spirit.***

How does the body aspect relate to your SAT prep? You can have knowledge and you may feel confident, but if your *energy level* falters, you will not be able to do your best on the SAT. Do you see how mind/body/spirit inter-relate? Just as strength in one aspect can bolster the other two, a shortcoming in one area—such as the body—can weaken the other two. That's why your physical self and its relation to SAT success is an important topic to consider.

For me, the physical issue involved more than "bring snacks and something to drink to the test center." How do you manage the anxiety that occurs before and during the SAT? How do you prepare yourself for those long four hours that the SAT requires? How do you work at peak efficiency from the first question to the last? I'll relate how I solved these very important and often ignored issues. Then, using your intuition, you can set-up a body prep routine that will work best for you.

When I take tests like the SAT, I usually become apprehensive as test day approaches. Then, during the test, I tend to speed up and to lose focus. When I am stressed, my anxiety level can skyrocket and prevent my mind from working properly. This was the self-destructive cycle that impeded me on previous tests and which I was determined to solve.

I reflected on my strengths and weaknesses to discover clues. What was I doing right, and what was hurting my performance? The mind/knowledge aspect of my prep was always solid: I put in the time on my cards and on the review questions. I had the knowledge, but was not reaching a score that reflected that level of knowledge.

Confidence, I suspected, was the issue. Or, to be precise, a lack of confidence. Although the mind aspect of my prep was complete, there was some curious body/spirit dysfunction that sapped my strength, making me doubt myself.

Knowing that I needed to build my confidence and to stay calm, I set up a diet and exercise schedule. I minimized my intake of coffee, tea, cola, and sugar— stuff that would speed me up. I also established an exercise routine centered around basketball and lap swimming.

This diet and exercise schedule really helped me. I slept more soundly and got up in the morning feeling relaxed and energized. Ready to go!

By following this routine for the month before my test, I was able to manage my ***pre-exam anxiety***. Feeling stronger and more confident, I was able to work more effectively on my memory and review questions as test day approached.

When I entered the test center, I sensed that I was prepared as I could ever be. I felt strong and at ease. As a result, I did not become anxious and speed up when confronted by the first tricky question. I was able to remain calm and confident throughout the entire exam, taking it one question at a time. As I left the test center, I truly believed that I had performed well on the test. I didn't need to see the score to confirm that I had been more successful. I just knew it.

Mind, body, and spirit inter-relate in curious and mysterious ways that differ from one person to another. It's important for you to understand their inter-relationship for yourself. Once you do, you can more easily pinpoint any issues that need to be addressed…whether in mind, body, or spirit. ***Assess your strengths and weaknesses; then, direct your energies to solving any shortcomings that might be impacting your performance on the SAT.***

For example, some of my students are already exercising and maintaining healthy diets. Their energy level is up, they feel calm and focused. For these students, body/spirit may be fine but they may need to spend more time on the mind aspect of their prep: more memory work, more review questions, and more timed tests.

Other students may suffer from an issue similar to mine: being so focused on the mind that they neglect the body and the spirit. Everyone is different. ***Let your intuition guide you to discover what may be short-circuiting you.*** Quiet moments (for me, lap swimming) are the times my intuition speaks the loudest and the clearest. Find those quiet moments and listen. Your inner voice will guide you to the mind/body/spirit solution that works best for you.

If you suspect that there's a problem you cannot solve on your own, pay a visit to your guidance department, or conference with a trusted teacher. Talk it out! One helpful suggestion can make a big difference in your score. There's so much at stake for you when you take your SAT. Why not do all that you can to get yourself in sync?

Doesn't this make sense… that if you want to be most effective when you take the SAT, you will need to have your mind, body, and spirit operating at their highest possible levels? That you will want to enter the test center equipped with as much knowledge, stamina and confidence as you can muster? Your working at peak efficiency will give you the best shot on the SAT. Make that your goal: to be at your personal best…*in your peak form*… on SAT Saturday.

What is Your Definition of
Being Successful on Your SAT?
It's all about YOU

At the end of my SAT Prep class, I ask my students to write a couple of paragraphs on this topic: How would you define "Being successful on your SAT"?

Here's a list of the most common responses:

- A specific point score

- Enough points to get into my favorite college

- X points more than my prior SAT

Left to the imagination are other answers which are kept secret, unexpressed but nevertheless very real:

- A score that will please my parents

- A higher score than my classmate...you fill in the name

- A score that will impress my teacher...you fill in the name

Usually, one of my students will ask me for my answer to the question. I reply with this quote from renowned basketball Coach John Wooden, whose teams won ten NCAA championships during his final twelve years at UCLA, including seven national titles in a row:

> *Success is peace of mind, which is a direct result of self-satisfaction in knowing that you made the effort to do the best of which you are capable.*

Note that Coach Wooden didn't stress winning or a point total as a component of success. "I wanted the score to be a by-product of the preparation," Wooden said. Here's one of the NCAA's most celebrated and successful coaches defining success not as a won/lost record, but as a more fundamental truth: *peace of mind derived from knowing that you made the effort to do your best!*

John Wooden's definition of success is masterful. The celebrated coach is basically saying, "Do your prep work and you will find your reward." Don't waste time comparing yourself to others. Or fretting about what you might score on the SAT. Don't waste your energy trying to predict the essay topic. You can't predict what the creators of the SAT will throw at you. But, you can be prepared to deal with whatever they do throw at you.

That's the key to success on the SAT: your preparation. Work hard to prepare yourself in the fullest possible way: mind, body and spirit. From this robust preparation, you will derive knowledge and strength and confidence. You will be able to do the best job that you can on the SAT.

Then, as Coach Wooden would say, you can walk out of the test center with the peace of mind derived from the knowledge *that you gave it your all.*

APPENDICES

1. **Integer**

   Any number that does not contain either a fraction or a decimal.

   ...-5, -4, -3, -2, -1, 0, 1 ,2, 3, 4, 5...

   Note: integers can be negative, positive, or 0.

2. **Whole Number**

   0 and all the positive integers

   0, 1, 2, 3, 4, 5...

3. **Positive Number**

   Any number greater than 0

   Can be a fraction, decimal, or an integer

   Examples: ½   2   7.25   57

4. **Negative Number**

   Any number less than 0

   Can be a fraction, decimal, or an integer

   Examples: -5   -3.14   -½   -.0001

5.   Even /Odd

even - divisible by 2
no fraction, no decimal
all others are odd
even #... -6, -4, -2, 0, 2, 4, 6
Ex: 0 is even   2.2 is not even

An even number is an **integer** that is divisible by 2 with no remainder.

Examples: -6, -4, -2, 0, 2, 4, 6

Note: 2.2 is not an even number because (a) it's not an integer and (b) when you divide 2.2 by 2, there is a remainder (.2). Note: 0 **is** an even number.

6. Prime Number

A number that is divisible only by 1 and itself.

Examples are: 2, 3, 5, 7, 11, 13, 17, 19, 23, 29, 31, 37, 41, 43, 47, 53

Note: 1 is not a prime number. 2 is the only even prime number

Hint: memorize this progression of prime numbers so that you don't have to waste time figuring them out during the test.

7. **Digit and Place**

    Digits are the numbers 0 through 9 (0, 1,2,3,4,5,6,7,8,9).
    There are ten digits.
    Place refers to the position of the digits in a number.
    Example: for the number 901.67, the digit 9 is in the
    hundreds place and the digit 7 is in the hundredths place

8. **Consecutive Numbers**

    A series of numbers increasing in value, moving from left
    to right on the number line.
    Example: -3, -2,   -1, 0,   1

9. **Distinct Numbers**

    The word *distinct* means different.
    Note: Unless the SAT specifies that terms are distinct,
    they can be the same.
    Example: x, y, and z are integers. Can xyz = 1?
    Yes: If x=1, y=1, and z=1 , then $1 \times 1 \times 1 = 1$
    Example: x, y and z are distinct integers. Can xyz = 1? No.

10. **Divisible by**

    A number that can be divided evenly by another number.
    Example: 12 is divisible by 1 and 12, 2 and 6, 3 and 4.
    1,2,3,4,6 and 12 are the positive integer factors of 12.

11. **Sum**

    The result of addition.
    When you see the word *sum*, know that you have to add.
    Find the sum of 2, 4, 6. Simply add: 2+4+6= 12

12. Difference

The result of subtraction

When the SAT asks you for the **difference**, know that you have to subtract.

Example A. What is the difference between 12 and 7?

Answer: 12 - 7 = 5

Example B. What is the difference between π and –π?

Answer π - (-π) = 2 π

13. Product

The result of multiplication

As soon as you see the word **product** in a math question, prepare to multiply.

Example: What is the product of 12 and 7?

Answer: 12 × 7 = 84

14. Quotient

The answer to a division question. When you divide 6 by 2, the **quotient** is 3.

Note: when 14 is divided by 4, the quotient is 3.5 and the **remainder** is 2. 14 ÷ 4 = 3 remainder 2

Know that the remainder in this division problem is 2… not .5 *The remainder is the amount that is left- over, without alteration.*

15. Set

A collection of elements or members.

Union: symbol is ∪

Intersection: symbol is ∩

A **union** of two sets includes **all** terms that appear in each set; an **intersection** of two sets includes only those terms that appear in **both** sets. See an example on the card that follows.

---

15. Set= collection of elements, members, terms

U= union - all
∩= intersection - only common terms
(must appear in both sets)

Set A= 0, π, 7 and Set B= -π, 0, 4, 7, 9
U Set A, B= -π, 0, π, 4, 7, 9
∩ Set A, B= 0, 7

16-A. The Rules of 0

0 is neither positive nor negative

is the only number that is equal to its opposite

is even

$0/X = 0$

$X/0$ is undefined. Cannot have 0 in the denominator

0 raised to any power = 0

16-B. The Rules of 1

1 is odd

is NOT a prime number

is the smallest positive integer

is a divisor of every integer $1^n = 1$

$x^0 = 1$ for any value x except if x = 0

17. Order of Operations—PEMDAS

Work in this order:

Parenthesis

Exponents

Multiplication and Division from left to right

Addition and Subtraction from left to right

Example:

$(2 + 4)\ 2 - 5 =$

$6 \times 2 - 5 =$

$12 - 5 = 7$

18. Absolute Value

Absolute Value is expressed as two parallel
vertical line segments | |.

It is always *positive*.

$$|\text{-}5| = 5$$
$$|5| = 5$$

It can also be defined as the distance from 0 on the
number line. ***Distance is always positive*** because whether
you move from 0 to the left by 5 feet… or from 0 to the
right by 5 feet… you have moved the *same* distance: 5
feet.

19. GCF and LCM

GCF = Greatest Common Factor

LCM = Least Common Multiple

To find GCF, draw a factor tree and multiply the *smallest*
number of primes that appear in *both* numbers.

To find LCM, use the same factor tree, then multiply the
greatest number of primes that appear in *each* number.

Example (Page 418 of *Barron's*) To find GCF and LCM of 108 and 240, first factor these numbers.

$108 = 2 \times 2 \times 3 \times 3 \times 3$

$240 = 2 \times 2 \times 2 \times 2 \times 3 \times 5$

GCF = $2 \times 2 \times 3$ (smallest number of primes that appear in both numbers) = 12

LCM = $2 \times 2 \times 2 \times 2 \times 3 \times 3 \times 3 \times 5$ (greatest number of primes that appear in each number)=2160

NOTE: Given two numbers x, y, their product

$$\mathbf{x \times y = GCF \times LCM}$$

Example: $108 * 240 = 12 * 2160 = 25{,}920$

20. Percent

Percent means "per hundred."

Example: What percent of b is a?

Next step: re-express as "What part of b is a?"

Final step: solve for x, where x = percent

$$a / b = x / 100$$

Example: What percent of 5 is 2?

Re-express as what part of 5 is 2?

Solve for x/100

$2/5 = x/100 \qquad x = 40\%$

Example: What percent of 5 is ★

Re-express as what part of 5 is ★ , then solve for x percent.

$★/5 = x/100$

$x = 100★ / 5 = 20★\%$

21. Reciprocal

The *reciprocal* of any non-zero number a = 1/a.

Note: the product of a and its reciprocal = 1

$a \times (1/a) = 1$

22. Exponents and Roots

$$b^m \times b^n = b^{m+n}$$

$$b^m \div b^n = b^{m-n}$$

$$(b^m)^n = b^{m \times n}$$

$$b^m \times c^m = (bc)^m$$

$$\sqrt{ab} = \sqrt{a} \times \sqrt{b}$$

$$\sqrt{a/b} = \sqrt{a} / \sqrt{b}$$

$$b^{-n} = 1 / b^n$$

$$b^{n/d} = \sqrt[d]{b^n}$$

Note: if $x^2 = 16$, $x = 4$ or $x = -4$

$\sqrt{16} = 4$ *always* positive root 4…not -4

$-4^2 = -16$ PEMDAS specifies that you perform power first, then multiply by -1.

This equation says $-1 \times 4^2 = -1 \times 16 = -16$

$(-4)^2 = 16$ because this equation indicates

$(-4) \times (-4) = 16$

$\sqrt{(a^2)}$ does not necessarily equal a because a can be negative

Example: $\sqrt{(-4)^2} = \sqrt{16} = 4$ (not -4)

23. Factorial

$n! = n$ factorial

Example: $4! = 4 \times 3 \times 2 \times 1 = 24$

$5! = 5 \times 4 \times 3 \times 2 \times 1 = 120$

Example: $(5!) - (4!) = 120 - 24 = 96$

24. Ratio

A ratio is expressed as x:y, or as x to y.

Example: The ratio of girls to boys in physics class is 3:2. What percent of the class are girls?

Solution: Create "**Ratio Box**" like this:

Girls	Boys	Total
3	2	5

Percent girls = 3/5 = x/100

Solve for x

x = 60%

25. Percent Increase/Decrease

Percent Increase and Decrease =
change ÷ initial amount

Example: What is the percentage increase in price when a computer that used to cost $1000 now costs $1100?

change = + $100   initial price = $1000

$100/$1000 = 1/10 = 10%

Example: What is the percentage decrease when a computer that used to cost $1100 now sells for $1000

Change = −$100   initial price $1100 =

% change = -$100/$1100 = −1/11 = −9 1/11 %

or − 9.09%

26. Direct / Inverse Relationship

Direct: y = kx, where k is a constant.

For *direct* relationships, if one number increases, so does the other, in the same proportion.

Example: if k = 2, when x doubles, y also doubles.

Inverse: xy = k   If one number increases, the other will decrease in the same proportion.

Example: if x doubles, then y will half.

27. **Average**

Three kinds of averages:

Average (arithmetic mean) = Total / Number

Example: Average of 5, 6 and 7 = 18 /3 = 6

Median – the number in the middle of a sequence

Example: find median of 2, 3, **4,** 5, 6 Answer: **4**

Example: find median of 2, 3, **4, 5**, 6, 7

When there are an even number of terms in a sequence, to find the median, you have to *average* the two middle numbers. (4 + 5) / 2 = **4.5**

Mode is the number that appears the most.

In this set, (2, 2, 2, 3, 4, 5), the mode is **2**.

28. **Factoring**

$(x + y)^2 = x^2 + 2xy + y^2$

$(x - y)^2 = x^2 - 2xy + y^2$

$(x + y) \times (x - y) = x^2 - y^2$

Hint: If you see the equation expressed one way, re-express it the other way to arrive at solution.

Example: If you see $x^2 - 25$, re-express this as $(x + 5) \times (x - 5)$. This new expression may lead you to the answer.

29. **System of Equations**

Here is how to add/subtract a system of equations.

First, line up the terms so that the powers are in the same column. Then, add/subtract as usual.

Example: What is the sum of $(2x^2 + 3x + 10)$ and $(-x^2-4x +5)$?

Solution: You see the word ***sum***, and know this means you have to add. Line up terms, and then add.

$$2x^2 + 3x + 10$$
$$-x^2 - 4x + 5$$
$$\overline{}$$
$$x^2 - x + 15$$

30. Inequalities

> greater than   ≥ greater than or equal to

< less than   ≤ less than or equal to

Note: if $x < y$, then $-x > -y$. When you change the sign of the terms, then you must reverse the inequality sign as well.

31. Distance Formulas

d = distance   r = rate   t = time

$d = r \times t$

$r = d / t$

$t = d / r$

Hint: be sure to ***keep terms consistent*** throughout your work. For example, if you are working in hours, to be consistent, covert minutes to hours before you plug numbers into the formulas.

32. **Angles**

    acute < 90° **right** = 90° **obtuse** > 90 °

    straight angle = line = 180 °

    circle contains 360 °

    Angles that add-up to 90° are *complementary.*

    Angles that add-up to 180° are *supplementary.*

    Vertical angles are equal   ><

33. **Triangles**

    Interior angles total 180°

    Isosceles contains two equal sides with their opposite angles equal.

    Equilateral triangle has three equal sides with three equal angles of 60°.

    Right triangle has one 90° angle.

    Scalene triangle has three unequal sides and three unequal angles

    Remember: *Longest side of triangle is opposite the biggest angle.*

Note: exterior angle of triangle – sum of two opposite interior angles. Know this! See math review section J2 in *Barron's.*

34. Triangle Inequality

sum of lengths of any 2 sides >
length of third side

a

b

c

ab + bc > ac
Remember: the shortest distance between
2 points is a straight line

Sum of lengths of two sides of a triangle is always **greater** than the length of the third side. Draw a triangle for proof. Line segment ac will always be shorter than (ab + bc) because the **shortest distance from a to c is a straight line.**

35. Right Triangle
Pythagorean Theorem $a^2 + b^2 = c^2$

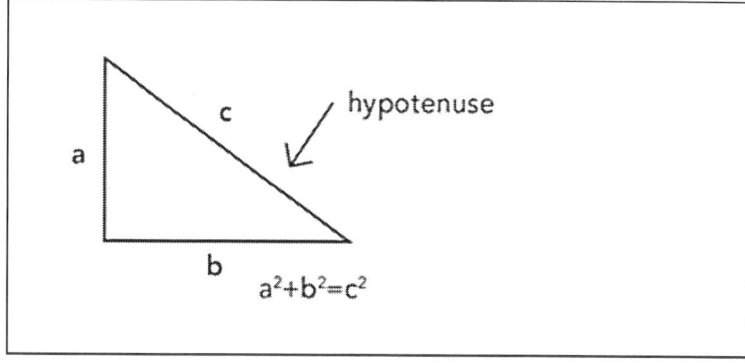

hypotenuse

c

a

b

$a^2 + b^2 = c^2$

36. Isosceles Right Triangle

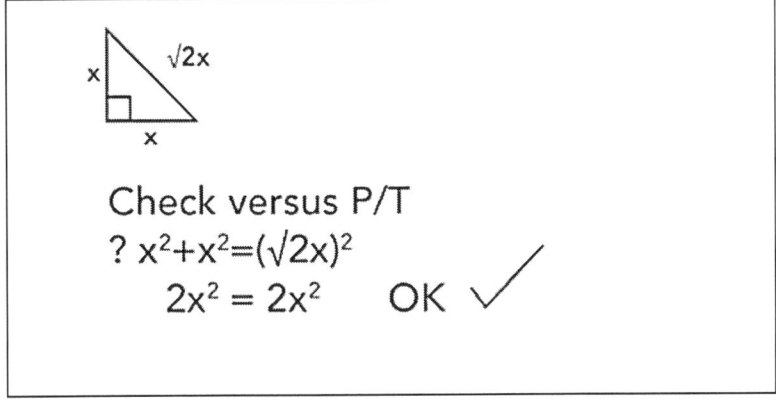

Check versus P/T
$? \ x^2+x^2=(\sqrt{2}x)^2$
$2x^2 = 2x^2$ OK ✓

Has right angle and two 45° angles. Sides opposite 45° angles are same length.

If sides are length x, hypotenuse is length √2x

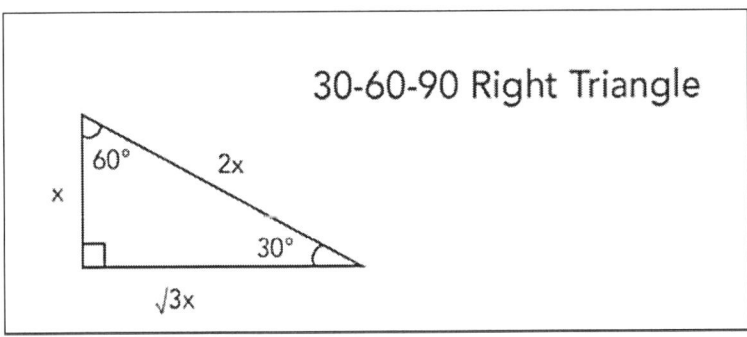

37. 30-60-90 Right Triangle

Side opposite 30° angle is length **x** Hypotenuse is **2x**, *twice as long as smallest side.* Side opposite 60° angle is √**3 x**

38. 3-4-5 Right Triangle

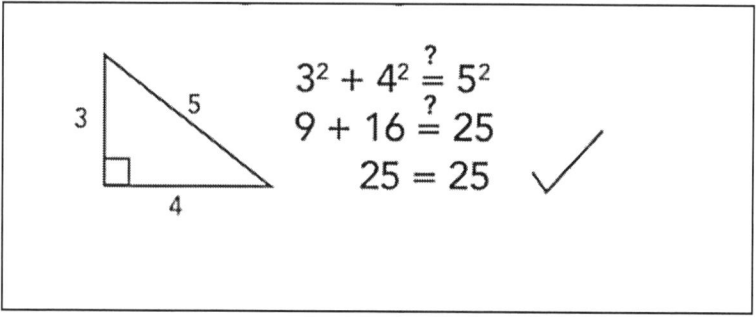

Also works with **multiples** of sides 3–4-5.

Multiply 3-4-5 by 2 and then sides will be 6-8-10.

39. Triangle Area and Perimeter

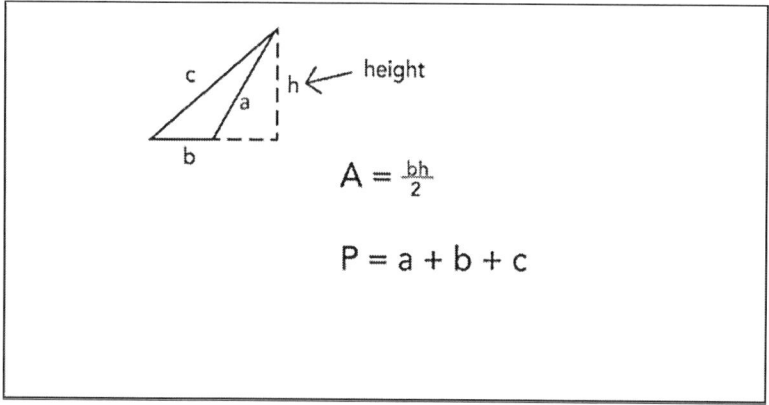

A = area b= base h = height A = (b × h) ÷ 2 or ½ (b × h)

Note that h has to be perpendicular to the base.

Perimeter: to find perimeter, simply add the lengths of the three sides. **P** = a + b + c

40. Polygon

A polygon is a figure with more than two sides.

- triangle is a 3-sided polygon
- quadrilateral (rectangle and squares) 4- sides
- pentagon 5-sides
- hexagon 6-sides
- heptagon 7-sides
- octagon 8-sides

Formula: A polygon of n sides has interior angles that measure
$(n-2) \times 180°$

Example: Triangle has three sides. Its interior angles measure:
$(3 - 2) \times 180° = 180°$

A pentagon has five sides. Its interior angles would measure
$(5-2) \times 180° = 3 \times 180° = 540°$

Note: exterior angles of all polygons measure 360°.

See *Barron's* math review Section K for a clear and illustrated explanation.

41. Parallelogram

Parallelograms are quadrilaterals: 4-sided

- opposite sides are parallel
- diagonals bisect
- consecutive angles = 180° (they are supplementary)
- opposite angles are equal

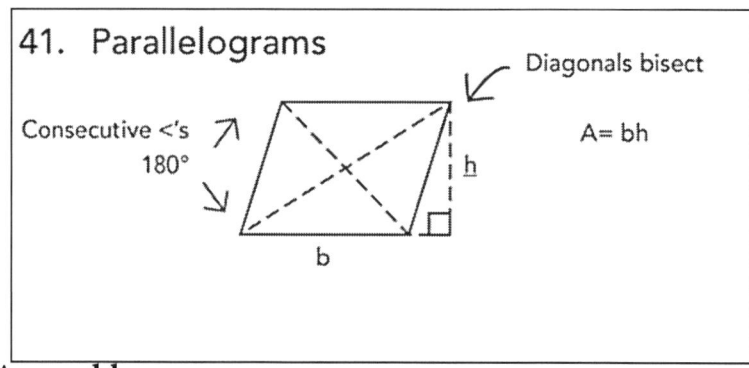

Area = bh

* Be sure to draw your height *perpendicular* to base.

Note distinction between height and side.

42. Rectangle/Square

Rectangles are quadrilaterals. Squares are rectangles with four equal sides. Not all rectangles are squares; but all squares are rectangles.

For a given perimeter, the rectangle with the greatest area is a square. For a given area, the rectangle with the greatest perimeter is not a square.

Hint: on the SAT, draw "weird" rectangles for the hardest math problems.

Example, below: Areas of the rectangle and square are both 36, but perimeters are very different

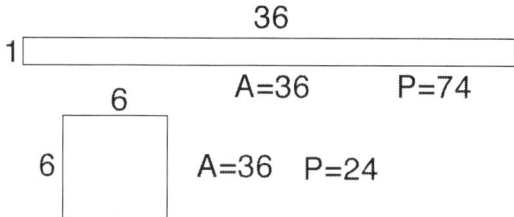

43. Circles

Contain 360°

$A = \pi r^2$

$D = 2r$

$C = \pi D$ and $C = 2\pi r$

$\pi = C/D = 3.14$ This formula shows you that π is the ratio of the circumference to the diameter. For most math SAT questions, you can solve *without converting* π to 3.14.

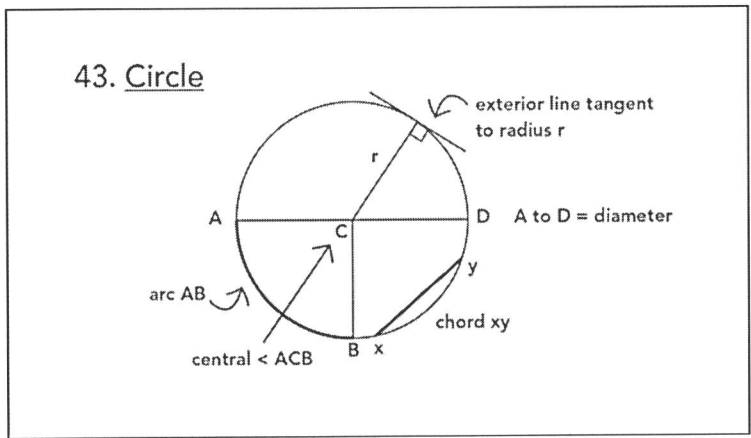

Chords are line segments drawn inside the circle.

The *longest chord* is the diameter.

An *arc* is a section of the circumference. The length of an arc is in the same proportion to the total circumference as its central angle° is to 360°.

You compute the *area of a sector* a circle the same way: central angle° of the sector/360 ° × area of the entire circle = area of a sector

Know this: A line drawn outside the circle that is tangent to a radius forms a right angle with the radius.

44. Solids

Volume formulas for solids are:

Rectangular: $V = l \times w \times h$

Cube : $V = s^3$

Cylinder: $V = \pi r^2 h$

Sphere: $V = 4/3 \, \pi r^3$

Hint: get a cereal box and count the *faces*, or sides. There are 6.

Also count the *vertices*, which are the 8 points where the sides meet.

For a cylinder, note that the volume is simply the area of the circle at the top (or bottom) multiplied by the height of the cylinder: $A = \pi r2 \times h$

Take a look at a cylindrical glass or tube, for example, to get a visual feel for the area of a cylinder.

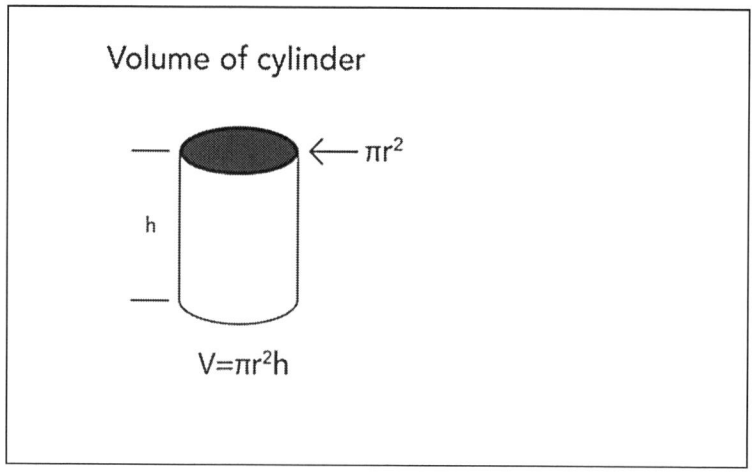

Volume of cylinder

πr^2

h

$V = \pi r^2 h$

45. Venn Diagrams

Use Venn Diagrams for math problems that have sets with intersecting members.

Example: Central High offers courses in two foreign languages: French and Spanish. There are 100 students in the junior class. 45 of them study French, 60 study Spanish, and 15 do not study either language. How many juniors study **both** French and Spanish?

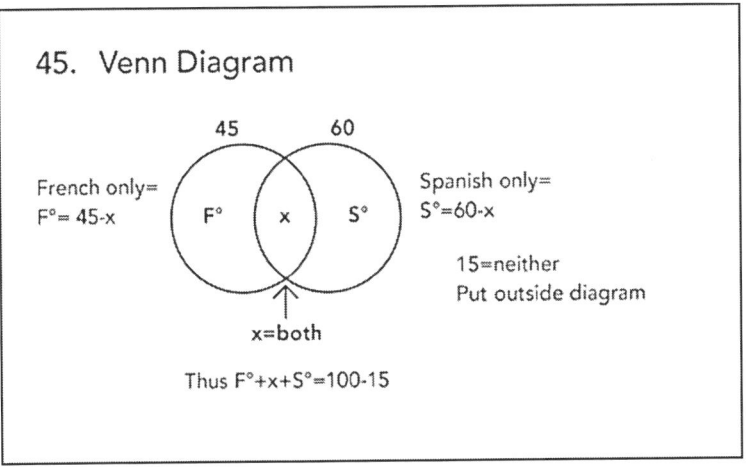

Solve for x:

45-x + x + 60-x = 100 − 15

105 − x = 85

x = 20

46. Co-ordinate geometry

Slope = rise over run or $(y^2 - y^1) \div (x^2 - x^1)$

Lines that are parallel have *same* slopes.

Lines that are perpendicular have ***negative reciprocal*** slopes.

Example: If Line A has slope of 2, a line perpendicular to it would have slope of -½. When you multiply slopes of two perpendicular lines, their product is -1

Horizontal lines have slope of **0.**

Vertical lines have ***undefined*** slope because you cannot have 0 in the denominator. (See *Barron's* math review Section N)

Formula: $y = mx + b$

m is the slope and **b** is the y-intercept when you plug-in 0 for x.

Lines that *rise* from left to right have + slope and m will be positive.

Lines that *fall* from left to right have – slope and m will be negative.

47. Probability

Probability ranges from 0 to 1.

O indicates *impossibility; 1* indicates *certainty.*

Formula for probability

number of *favorable* outcomes/number of **possible** outcomes.

Example: When you flip a coin, what is probability of heads?

Probability = ½ because there is one head (favorable) divided by two possible outcomes (head + tail).

Probability of 2 consecutive heads = ½ × ½ = ¼

Probability of 3 consecutive heads = ½ × ½ × ½ = ⅛

48. Permutation/Combination

A *permutation* refers to an arrangement of items (numbers, letters, people, paintings, etc.) in a certain order. To compute, take number of items n and compute n! .

Example: You have five model train cars. How many ways can you line them up?

Answer: 5 ! = 5 × 4 × 3 × 2 × 1 = 120 ways.

A *combination* is an arrangement in which order does not matter.

Example: Pizza Galore offers 10 pizza toppings. You can choose any of 3 of them. How many possible combinations are there?

Solution: (10 × 9 × 8) / (3 × 2 × 1) = 120 combinations

See *Barron's* math review Section O, Princeton Review Part III (around Page 235), or College Board Math Review Page 241.

49. Domain and Range

Domain is the set of real numbers that can be plugged-into a function. On the SAT, you cannot have a number in the domain that would create 0 in the denominator (cannot divide by 0) or put a negative number in a square root box (cannot take square root of a negative number).

Range is the set of all real numbers that result from a calculation.

In formula y = f (x), the x would be your domain (what you plug-in) and the y would be the range (the result of your calculation).

50. Transformations

Given a graph of the function $y = f(x)$, here is what would happen if you altered the formula.

$y = f(x) + r$ graph would move UP r units

$y = f(x) - r$ graph would move DOWN r units

$y = f(x + r)$ graph would move LEFT by r units

$y = f(x - r)$ graph would move RIGHT by r units

$y = - f(x)$ graph would turn upside down

See excellent examples in *Barron's* Math Review Section R, Princeton Review Math Review around Page 261, and College Board Math Section around Page 259.

APPENDIX B: KEY NUMBERS AND CONVERSIONS
Memorize them to save time on your SAT

---

1. Key Numbers

    $\pi \cong 3.14$

    $\sqrt{2} \cong 1.4$

    $\sqrt{3} \cong 1.7$

2. Convert fractions to decimals to percents for the following fractions: halves, thirds, quarters, fifths and eights.

    Here is how to set up the conversions. Note: since you can reduce fractions like 2/4 and 4/8 to ½, these do not appear in the table.

$\frac{1}{2} = .5 = 50\%$	$\frac{3}{5} = .6 = 60\%$
$\frac{1}{3} = .33\frac{1}{3} = 33\frac{1}{3}\%$	$\frac{4}{5} = .8 = 80\%$
$\frac{2}{3} = .66\frac{2}{3} = 66\frac{2}{3}\%$	$\frac{1}{8} = .125 = 12\frac{1}{2}\% = 12.5\%$
$\frac{1}{4} = .25 = 25\%$	$\frac{3}{8} = .375 = 37\frac{1}{2}\% = 37.5\%$
$\frac{3}{4} = .75 = 75\%$	$\frac{5}{8} = .625 = 62\frac{1}{2}\% = 62.5\%$
$\frac{1}{5} = .2 = 20\%$	$\frac{7}{8} = .875 = 87\frac{1}{2}\% = 87.5\%$
$\frac{2}{5} = .4 = 40\%$	

3. Memorize powers of 2, 3, 4, and 5. Here are some examples:

$2^2 = 4$ $2^3 = 8$ $2^4 = 16$ $2^5 = 32$

$2^6 = 64$ $2^7 = 128$ $2^8 = 256$

$3^2 = 9$ $3^3 = 27$ $3^4 = 81$ $3^5 = 243$

$4^2 = 16$ $4^3 = 64$ $4^4 = 256$

$5^2 = 25$ $5^3 = 125$ $5^4 = 625$

4. PRIME Numbers: memorize them from 2 up to 53, as listed on math card # 6

---

6. Prime Number

= divisible only by 1 and itself

2, 3, 5, 7, 11, 13, 17, 19, 23, 29, 31, 37, 41, 43, 47, 53

*Note: 1 is **not** a prime number
2 is only even prime number

APPENDIX C. KEY WEIGHTS AND MEASURES
Memorize and Visualize these Terms

12 inches = 1 foot

3 feet = 1 yard

1760 yards = 5280 feet = 1 mile

2 cups = 1 pint

1 pint = 16 ounces

A pint's a pound the world around.

2 pints = 1 quart = 32 ounces

4 quarts = 1 gallon

16 ounces = 1 pound

2000 pounds = 1 ton

60 seconds = 1 minute

60 minutes = 1 hour

24 hours = 1 day

Clock: Visualize as a circle. ***Hour hand moves 30° per hour. Minute hand moves 360° per hour, or 30° every five minutes.***

At 3 o'clock, the hour and minute hands form a 90° angle (three 30° angles). At 3:10, the hands form a 35° angle because (1) the minute hand distance from 2 to 3 = 30° and (2) the hour hand has advanced 10 minutes = 1/6 hours×30° per hour=5°. Thus, 3:10 creates a 35° angle.

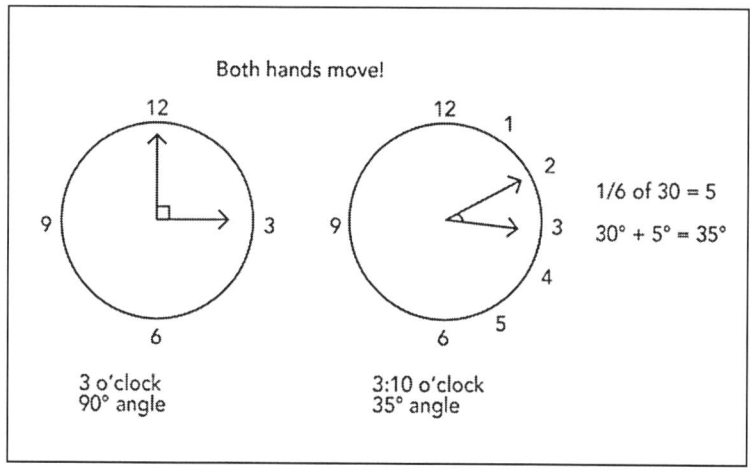

Calendar: Memorize this phrase: 30 days has September, April, June, and November. All the rest have 31, except for February, which has 28.

Note: February has 29 days in a **Leap Year**, which equals 366 days.

Directions North (up) South (down) East (right) West (left)

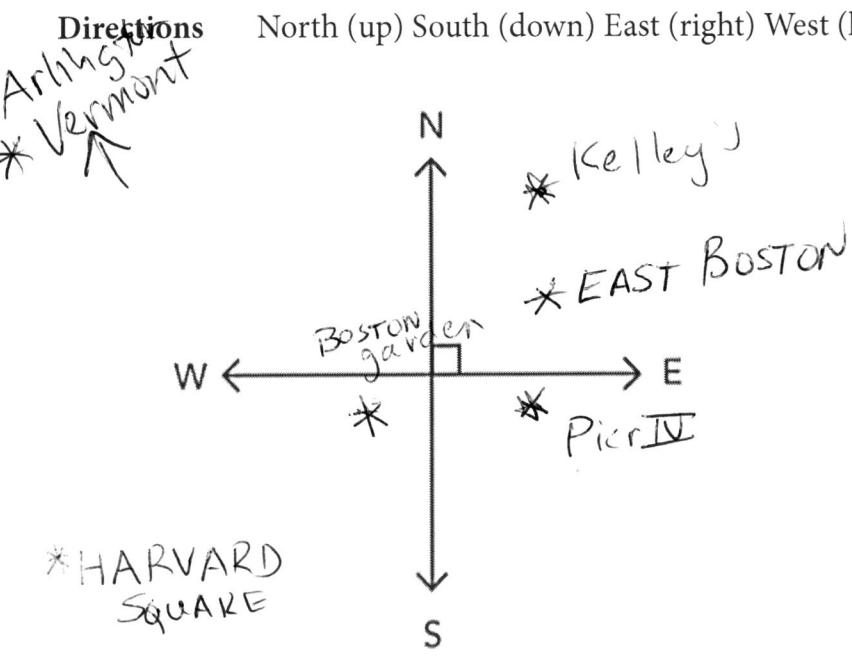

Arlington
* Vermont

N

* Kelley

* EAST BOSTON

BOSTON garden

W ←————————————→ E

*

* Pier IV

* HARVARD SQUARE

S

Example: Mary is practicing for an upcoming marathon. From starting Point S, she runs 2 miles north, then 3 miles east, and then 6 miles south. After running these 11 miles, how far is Mary located from her starting point S?

<u>Catalyst</u>= draw diagram

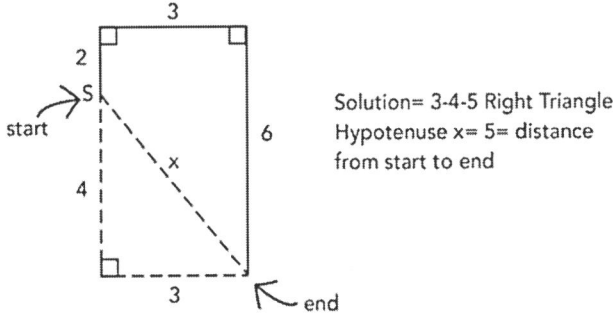

3

2

S
start

6

x

4

3

end

Solution= 3-4-5 Right Triangle
Hypotenuse x= 5= distance
from start to end

ACKNOWLEDGMENTS

Many thanks to my MS Word instructor, Linda Zukauskas, whose encouragement kept me on course as I started this project.

Marisa LaFleur was of great assistance in cleaning-up the illustrations. Her diligent work transformed my primitive hand-written diagrams into clear illustrations.

My daughter Christine Cascella and Elizabeth Veillette were tenacious editors. They kept me focused on topic and restrained my penchant for inserting too many quotes from Sherlock Holmes.

Kim Thwaits deftly designed the front and back covers with a distinctive, upbeat style that conveys the spirit of *Inverse the Curse*.

Many thanks to Catherine Larson, whose prolific design skills lent coherence and clarity to the final edit.

Finally, my wife, Teri, and my daughters, Ann and Christine, urged me to keep moving forward and to get the job done. Thanks so much for all your support along the way!

Made in the USA
Charleston, SC
14 July 2014